GOOD PASTURE

ROPE MYERS

WE WERE MADE FOR HIGHER GROUND

WHAT OTHERS ARE SAYING ABOUT THIS BOOK

Rope Myers' story is an inspiration of what God can do in a person's life when you give him the reins and let Him lead. Rope is a champion not just in the rodeo arena but also in the eyes of God as a son, husband, father, and friend. I recommend "Good pasture" for anyone who wants to be inspired to lead a life of obedience and trust in God."

Chad Hennings
Founder of Wingmen Ministries,
3-Time Super Bowl Champion,
Former Air Force A-10 Fighter Pilot

"World class rodeo cowboy, TV star, son, husband, father, and friend, Rope Myers has hit-a-lick with Good Pastures. It is not just his championship buckles and envious resume, but his amazing display of real deal, real man, leather-tough authenticity. Rope walks the reader through a behind the curtains look at the heart of a man who, by all standards is a Man's Man. Instead of the predictable, aloof, quintessential strong-silent cowboy, Rope shows his true strength early and continues to throughout the entire book. He is soaked in Cowboy culture and dares to break the expected stereotype into something even stronger; A real-deal cowboy tough enough to have a heart and share it with us. Loaded with Biblical reference points and summarized by lessons learned this is a great read for anyone looking for a role model or ready to break out to a higher level of faith, family and life. As for Susie and me, Rope's already high stock went up after this read. Nod your head, hold on and let Good Pastures take you for a ride."

Mark Eaton & Susie McEntire-Eaton
Eaton Leadership Foundation
Host of Cowboy Church TV
Pastor, CornerStone Church
Award Winning Vocalist

Published by

Burkhart *Books*
www.BurkhartBooks.com
Bedford , Texas

DEDICATION

To Candice

I have no story to tell without the Father
and I wouldn't know the Father had He not led me to you.

CONTENTS

FOREWORD

Everyone has a story, and each of them is worth knowing. Sometimes, however, you run across one that shouts truth so loudly that you are never the same afterward. Rope Myers' story has that kind of impact. It would be tragic if not told and sad if it is not heard. I am so glad he took the pains to make it accessible to all of us.

In God's gracious plan, Rope's story is highlighted on a big stage with lots of people watching. The professional rodeo world reflects a part of our history that connects with our collective soul. Few of us can rope and ride like those cowboys and cowgirls, but we wish we could, and admire those who do. We have only a small idea of the pressures and processes of that world. This story will give you a better glimpse into that world, but even more an open view of God's patient, persistent love pursuing and capturing his own.

You'll identify with the struggles, disappointments, and victories, and you'll be encouraged that God loves you with the same passion that won the heart of this World Champion Cowboy. I remember watching Rope in the arena with jaw-dropping awe. I've also watched him loving and mentoring kids with the same passion he once displayed on his horse. He is still a champion as he gives his life for others to the glory of God. That is something we can all do.

Dudley Hall
Author, Teacher, Speaker,
President Kerygma Ventures

THE GOOD SHEPHERD AND HIS SHEEP

I tell you the truth, anyone who sneaks over the wall of a sheepfold, rather than going through the gate, must surely be a thief and a robber! But the one who enters through the gate is the shepherd of the sheep. The gatekeeper opens the gate for him, and the sheep recognize his voice and come to him. He calls his own sheep by name and leads them out. After he has gathered his own flock, he walks ahead of them, and they follow him because they know his voice. They won't follow a stranger; they will run from him because they don't know his voice.

Yes, I am the gate. Those who come in through me will be saved. They will come and go freely and will find good pastures. The thief's purpose is to steal and kill and destroy. My purpose is to give them a rich and satisfying life.

INTRODUCTION

This book is my attempt to show how my Shepherd has led me. My hope is it will help you to hear His voice and to follow Jesus to the new good pasture He has made especially for you. I have written the story with a section following each chapter trying to show some of the lessons the Father has shown me. Many of these lessons I didn't learn until much later; some I am still trying to learn. My Father is patient though, and He has this gentle way of leading us. In hindsight, I think that God was more concerned with spending time with me than teaching me. More to the point, God gave me these opportunities to spend time with Him.

I have written it in three parts that run concurrently. The first I call the story. This is simply what happened. It includes the emotions and revelations that happened in either real time or shortly after the experience. In these sections, I tried to recall the exact frame of reference that held me in the moment and tried to filter out thoughts and ideas about the events that arrived later.

The second section I am calling Good Pasture. This is an allegorical view of the way the Father was consciously or at least semi-consciously leading me on the journey to find the light and life He had always intended for me to have and lead. It is a parable of how I see my story being told from a more heavenly perspective.

The third section in each chapter I refer to as "what I learned later" is filled with some of the many lessons, principles and axioms the Father has shown me at a much later date by anchoring truths God revealed to me through experiences that happened at other times in my life.

I am not a scholar or a theologian, so I hold out no claim that the doctrines are inerrant. I only know that at this point in my life this is the way I know my Father, Jesus, and the Holy Spirit. My pastor says we should be careful not to tie up the ends on what we think we know, and my hope is your mind will be open to taking anything in this book that is of value in your walk with the Father to the Good Pasture He has perfectly made for you.

CHAPTER 1

*... and other sheep I have which are not of this fold; them
also I must bring, and they will hear My voice; and there will
be one flock with one shepherd.*

John 10:16

Funny thing about my path to the Good Shepherd, it actually
began with a bunch of goats.

BUT THE VERY HAIRS OF YOUR HEAD ARE ALL NUMBERED.

As a 12-year-old boy growing up with a father who was a rodeo
cowboy, I was often asked if I had a choice about whether I wanted
to rodeo or not. My answer has often been every kid likes to play
cowboys and Indians; I was just fortunate enough to be able to
use real horses. When I was small my dad and mom were both
schoolteachers and they both competed in rodeos on the weekends.
So, we would leave Friday from school and travel to a rodeo on
Friday and Saturday night. For a young boy, it was an incredibly
fun adventure. I would mimic the announcer, pal around with
the rodeo clowns, and strap my miniature Larry Mahan bareback
rigging to the bleachers and ride every horse for all I was worth.

Each summer I would get to travel all over the country with
my parents going to different towns and cities, riding carnival
rides, swimming in hotel swimming pools, and eating concession
stand food. All things boys love! I got to fly paper airplanes out
of the upper deck at the Pontiac Superdome, go to Disneyland,
and swim in the Gulf of Mexico. My parents were hard-working
middle-class people as were most of my friends at school, but
rodeo allowed us to have opportunities that were usually reserved
for people of more means.

Through this world of rodeo I met amazing men like Tee
Woolman who would rope the team roping dummy with me, guys

like Mike and Scotty Fletcher who would let me sit in their saddle bronc saddles and practice my spur stroke and bull riders Jerry Beagley and Bobby DelVecchio who would let me watch them tie on their gloves and boots before going out to ride. With those opportunities, it wasn't surprising I wanted to compete as soon as I was able. It began with being able to enter the calf scrambles at the rodeos my dad competed at. I was usually smaller than the other kids trying to get the ribbon, but I was always packing my rope. At one such rodeo after a kid cut me off and grabbed the ribbon, I decided to just rope the kid. Soon I was entering the calf riding, and before long I entered my first junior rodeo, the Kansas City Fellowship of Police rodeo at the old Benjamin Stables. I had waited my whole life for this. I was entered in the cow riding, the breakaway roping, goat tying, and the barrel race. We arrived at rodeo, and it rained all night. The arena was a sloppy, muddy mess, but I was entered, and I was excited. My first event cow riding didn't go so well. I rode her about three jumps and tried to jump onto the clown as we flew by him. Later, I missed my calf, got terribly muddy in the goat tying, and was too slow in the barrel race, but I was hooked. Afterward, I was entering everything my parents would let me go to. By the time I was 12, we were going to a lot of Little Britches rodeos, and my favorite event had become the boy's goat tying.

This is how I came to be in the goat pen in Skidmore, MO at seven am on a Sunday morning. I wanted to get a chance to tie the goats before everyone else was up, so I had gone to the pen to get some practice in. Upon arriving at the pen, though, I realized it was going to be difficult. The pen was directly behind the stands, and they were having a church service. Since goats aren't exactly quiet, I knew I would never be able to tie them with a church service happening 25 feet away. Now, it's not that I had anything against God or Church. My parents would often drop my sister and me off for Sunday school. My parents had no affinity for religion, but Sunday was the only day my dad would even consider sleeping in. Consequently, many times my mom, in her bathrobe, would drop my sister and I off at the tiny little church in our tiny town, and we would go to Sunday school. So, I wasn't against Church, but I was wishing they weren't having it so close to where the goats were. Since I couldn't tie the goats until the service was over, I decided I might as well go sit in the stands and see if I could learn something. That morning, for the first time, I realized that Jesus was not just a story from olden times, but He was alive, and He wanted to save me. I don't remember anything in particular about the message; all I really remember is when the preacher asked if anyone would like to know Jesus, they could raise their hands. I raised my hand. I believe the preacher prayed, they gave me a cowboy New Testament Bible, and I left. You know I never did tie any goats that morning.

> WHAT MAN OF YOU, HAVING A HUNDRED SHEEP, IF HE LOSES ONE OF THEM, DOES NOT LEAVE THE NINETY-NINE IN THE WILDERNESS, AND GO AFTER THE ONE WHICH IS LOST UNTIL HE FINDS IT? 5 AND WHEN HE HAS FOUND IT, HE LAYS IT ON HIS SHOULDERS, REJOICING. AND WHEN HE COMES HOME, HE CALLS TOGETHER HIS FRIENDS AND NEIGHBORS, SAYING TO THEM, 'REJOICE WITH ME, FOR I HAVE FOUND MY SHEEP WHICH WAS LOST!' I SAY TO YOU THAT LIKEWISE THERE WILL BE MORE JOY IN HEAVEN OVER ONE SINNER WHO REPENTS THAN OVER NINETY-NINE JUST PERSONS WHO NEED NO REPENTANCE. (LUKE 15:4-7)

GOOD PASTURE

The gatekeeper opens the gate for him, and the sheep recognize his voice and come to him. He calls his own sheep by name and leads them out.

John 10:3

Every journey has a beginning and hearing the Shepherd call me at this little rodeo bleacher church service was the beginning of mine. I was a lost sheep looking to tie some goats, but the Father knew I would be there, and He called me to Himself.

What I learned later

O LORD, you have examined my heart
  and know everything about me.
You know when I sit down or stand up.
  You know my thoughts even when I'm far away.
You see me when I travel
  and when I rest at home.
  You know everything I do.
You know what I am going to say
  even before I say it, LORD.
You go before me and follow me.
  You place your hand of blessing on my head.
Such knowledge is too wonderful for me,
  too great for me to understand!
I can never escape from your Spirit!
  I can never get away from your presence!
If I go up to heaven, you are there;
  if I go down to the grave, you are there.
If I ride the wings of the morning,
  if I dwell by the farthest oceans,
Even there your hand will guide me,
  and your strength will support me.
I could ask the darkness to hide me
  and the light around me to become night—
But even in darkness I cannot hide from you.
  To you the night shines as bright as day.
  Darkness and light are the same to you.
You made all the delicate, inner parts of my body
  and knit me together in my mother's womb.
Thank you for making me so wonderfully complex!
  Your workmanship is marvelous—how well I know it.
You watched me as I was being formed in utter
  seclusion, as I was woven together in the dark
  of the womb.

You saw me before I was born.
Every day of my life was recorded in your book.
Every moment was laid out
before a single day had passed.
How precious are your thoughts about me, [b] O God.
They cannot be numbered!
I can't even count them;
they outnumber the grains of sand!
And when I wake up,
you are still with me!
O God, if only you would destroy the wicked!
Get out of my life, you murderers!
They blaspheme you;
your enemies misuse your name.
O LORD, shouldn't I hate those who hate you?
Shouldn't I despise those who oppose you?
Yes, I hate them with total hatred,
for your enemies are my enemies.
Search me, O God, and know my heart;
test me and know my anxious thoughts.
Point out anything in me that offends you,
and lead me along the path of everlasting life.

Psalm 139

God always knew me, and He always loved me. He made me, and He placed me exactly where He wanted to. The Father knew I would be inspired by competition, by men who challenged themselves in the sport of rodeo. Jesus knew I would love my own dad, and I would aspire to be like him. Christ was the one who made me, so of course, He knew I would want to go tie those goats in Skidmore, Missouri. He knew that 12 was a perfect time to send some preacher to let me hear the Gospel on just that day. He drew me there by His Spirit and that Spirit knew me by name. Knew me so intimately that raising my hand seemed the most natural thing in the world. By the way, He knows you that intimately as well. Many of the "coincidences" that may have led to you an encounter with the Father happened because Jesus knows you so well. Times when you heard something that stuck in the back of your mind, moments when inspiration took hold of you, people God brought across your path, the activities you have enjoyed doing for recreation, even picking up and reading this book are evidence of the love the Father has for you and evidence that He knows your name.

CHAPTER 2

When I left Missouri that day, I knew very little about what had taken place in my heart, but the preacher did send me home with a Bible, and I love to read. I remember being sent to clean the trailer and make the beds. I saw the Bible, and I opened it up. As I flipped it open, I noticed some words were in Italics (this Bible had Jesus' words in Italics), so I started reading there. I had no history of reading the Bible except for a few Sunday school classes, mostly stuff like the names of the apostles, the story of Noah's ark, a little about Jesus dying on a cross, but no real understanding of any of that. However, as I began to read the words in italics, I was drawn into these stories. Stories of Jesus feeding people, healing people, and talking to them in a clear way by telling stories of farmers, fishermen, and other common people which made me feel like I was somehow a part of the story, too.

AND LET THE PEACE OF GOD RULE IN YOUR HEARTS, TO WHICH ALSO YOU WERE CALLED IN ONE BODY; AND BE THANKFUL.

I read some out of that Bible fairly regularly for the next six or seven months. At about the end of this period. My dad was invited to a World Cup rodeo event in Australia, and he was able to take our entire family with him for an entire two-week stay. It was one of the most amazing experiences not just because of the beautiful country, the incredible amount of fun, or the chance to be with my family on an adventure, there was something more. I had a peace within me, in my heart that felt almost palpable. Before this trip, my sister and I had always gotten along, but we were a year apart, and as any close siblings will do we would occasionally squabble. On this trip, there was none of that; we just had an incredible time together. I felt no want. Hamburgers that had beets on them were funny, not distressing. Pizzas that came almost automatically with anchovies were gross, but they weren't cause to be upset. At the time, of course, I didn't notice this, and I certainly didn't connect this in any way with the Father. However, six months or so later I would be angry or getting in trouble or just downright miserable and ask myself why I couldn't be "happy the way I was in Australia." Instead, I seemed to be getting more and more easily upset. I would find myself meeting some former friend on the corner after school to duke it out. I would be angry for no apparent reason. I began to feel insecure even around people I knew well. Of course, I realize this is common among teenagers, but there was always a sense within me that while hormones may have been a part of it that wasn't the whole story.

GOOD PASTURE

And as He walked by the Sea of Galilee, He saw Simon and Andrew his brother casting a net into the sea; for they were fishermen. Then Jesus said to them, "Follow Me, and I will make you become fishers of men." They immediately left their nets and followed Him. When He had gone a little farther from there, He saw James the son of Zebedee, and John his brother, who also were in the boat mending their nets. And immediately He called them, and they left their father Zebedee in the boat with the hired servants and went after Him.

Mark 1:16-20

Jesus had called me, and I had heard His call. Much like the disciples I didn't know the scope of the adventure I was being called to. During the beginning of any journey or quest the Leader calls and the followers begin following but they usually seem to be unaware of what is in store. (Gandalf retrieves the ring from the Shire and the Hobbits gainfully follow, blithely ignorant of the incredible adventure they were stepping into.) I too began following with no idea of the full scope of impact it would have on my life. I have a friend named Butch Bruton who says that this is grace- because if we knew the challenges that lie ahead we would never begin.

WHAT I LEARNED LATER

And He said, "The kingdom of God is as if a man should scatter seed on the ground, and should sleep by night and rise by day, and the seed should sprout and grow, he himself does not know how. For the earth yields crops by itself: first the blade, then the head, after that the full grain in the head. But when the grain ripens, immediately he puts in the sickle, because the harvest has come."

Mark 4:26-29

The Word is alive, and when we receive it even when we aren't trying to grow or change the Word has Kingdom power in itself. The mere action of receiving the Word allows it to produce in your life. First, the blade of grass comes up. The blade of grass doesn't resemble the seed. Then the flower or head is produced. We see the flower, and we think of beauty, but the power of the flower is that it is the mechanism for reproducing the seed. Later, after the flower has gone away, the plant produces the seed which bears the same power as the original seed. Finally, after the seed is fully mature it is time to harvest.

This is the same process that happens in our hearts whenever the Word is sown there. The Word becomes a blade (*sharper than any two-edged sword, piercing even to the division of soul and spirit*). The Word pierces the ground of our hearts and begins to grow toward the sun(son). As it receives Light and a little water soon it produces a bloom. This is similar to the bloom, or glow, or "something different" about the believer. Just like the plant the power is its ability to reproduce the life in the seed. In the same way, when I was in Australia my own family remarked several times about how great I had been on that trip. Finally, the seed or "fruit" matures. *The fruit of the Spirit is love, joy,* **peace**, *patience, kindness, goodness, and self-control.* Then it is time to harvest. In the same way the fruit on the apple tree is not for itself neither is the fruit in the believer's life for the believer. The fruit is for those that pass by the tree or the believer. If we don't put in the sickle to harvest the fruit may spoil on the vine. Likewise, when the Father produces this fruit of the Spirit in us we can share it with those around us. The power is that the seed is in the fruit. When we give away that fruit the seed can be planted anew.

Chapter 3

Like most teenagers when they feel like their world is a little shook, I looked around for what might stabilize it. So, I threw myself into pretty much everything I could. After all, if you can stay really busy you won't notice a nagging feeling in the pit of your gut. I went out for football as a 115-pound freshman. On the field, I kept throwing myself around so much that they let me start half-way through my sophomore season. I played basketball, not well, but as one with something to prove. I also made varsity as a sophomore. I tried nearly everything there was to try at school, from FFA to forensics meets, from student government to math competitions I was signed up and still not satisfied. Even though I was very successful at most of these things, winning math competitions, earning a gold medal at the State FFA contest, becoming student council president, I still felt something was missing.

"EVERYTHING IS MEANINGLESS," SAYS THE TEACHER, "COMPLETELY MEANINGLESS!" WHAT DO PEOPLE GET FOR ALL THEIR HARD WORK UNDER THE SUN? GENERATIONS COME AND GENERATIONS GO, BUT THE EARTH NEVER CHANGES. THE SUN RISES AND THE SUN SETS, THEN HURRIES AROUND TO RISE AGAIN. THE WIND BLOWS SOUTH, AND THEN TURNS NORTH, AROUND AND AROUND IT GOES, BLOWING IN CIRCLES. RIVERS RUN INTO THE SEA, BUT THE SEA IS NEVER FULL. THEN THE WATER RETURNS AGAIN TO THE RIVERS AND FLOWS OUT AGAIN TO THE SEA. 8 EVERYTHING IS WEARISOME BEYOND DESCRIPTION. NO MATTER HOW MUCH WE SEE, WE ARE NEVER SATISFIED. NO MATTER HOW MUCH WE HEAR, WE ARE NOT CONTENT. (ECCLESIASTES 1:2-8)

During this time, I can remember a spring afternoon in Kansas when the thunderheads were huge, and a storm was imminent. As I rode my horse out to the pasture to gather the steers, I remember thinking WOW God is sooooo big and sooooo powerful. It was a strange sense of awe and fear and wonder. A little before this I had heard someone say God scares me when you get Him indoors. As I was riding that day I thought about that quote, and I began to take it to heart. While my life was a bit out of tune, something about that ride felt holy, and I knew that God was real. I just wasn't ready to give Him my life yet.

I began to seek some less constructive ways to fill the hole I had begun to feel in my own chest. Girls became a distraction. They seemed to take my mind off my troubles. The problem was there weren't very many of them that would give me the time of day. The few that did certainly didn't last long. Either they were certain enough about themselves that they could soon see into my mess and wanted no part of it, or they were such a mess that I could tell that wasn't the way.

GOOD PASTURE

The thief's purpose is to steal and kill and destroy.
My purpose is to give them a rich and satisfying life.
John 10:10

When you won't follow the Shepherd, your life is open to the thief. Even the things I filled my life with only robbed my joy and left me feeling pretty dead inside. Without the Father in my life, all the activity only produced a deeper more gaping hole in my chest. Of course, the Father was aware of this, yet He patiently allowed me the space to find out for myself. He was always there though, providing little moments of clarity, like the one when I was riding my horse, to call me further down the path towards the good pasture where He wanted to lead me.

WHAT I LEARNED LATER

"Listen! Behold, a sower went out to sow. And it happened, as he sowed, that some seed fell by the wayside; and the birds of the air came and devoured it. Some fell on stony ground, where it did not have much earth; and immediately it sprang up because it had no depth of earth. But when the sun was up it was scorched, and because it had no root it withered away. And some seed fell among thorns; and the thorns grew

up and choked it, and it yielded no crop.
But other seed fell on good ground and yielded a crop
that sprang up, increased and produced: some thirty-fold,
some sixty, and some a hundred."

Mark 4:38

For as the rain comes down,
and the snow from heaven,
And do not return there,
But water the earth,
And make it bring forth and bud,
That it may give seed to the sower
And bread to the eater,
So shall My word be that goes forth from My mouth;
It shall not return to Me void,
But it shall accomplish what I please,
And it shall prosper in the thing for which I sent it.

Isaiah 55:10-11

Not all of the seed planted landed on good ground, and not all of the seed appeared to produce.

These two verses were some of the first verses that came alive to me more than ten years later when I began to share my faith at my steer wrestling clinics. There was a time when I saw the contrast between these two verses. In one it appears that the seed doesn't always produce (the parable of the sower) while in the other (Is 55:10) it says that the "word or seed does not return void, but it shall accomplish what the Lord pleases, and it (the seed) shall prosper in the thing for which I sent it." One day at one of my clinics these two verses connected for me in this way. I began to see that when I would give my students instructions (in other words sow seeds into their steer wrestling) it often would go in one ear and out the other when they first heard it. Like the birds of the air coming to take the seed (or instruction) from them. Then the Father reminded me of an odd ornithological fact that I had picked up somewhere. I had learned that as one of the biological adaptations for flight, birds have a very streamlined digestive tract and this detail causes birds to defecate when they take off for flight. So, in other words, when the birds of the air alight to steal the seed they fertilize the ground when they take off, preparing the ground for future seed. This parable would play out in my steer wrestling students. I would tell them something (sow the seed), it would be stolen (birds of the air); consequently, the next run wouldn't work. However, afterward the students would be more ready and able to receive the instruction. Therefore, the ground was better for the seed having been there. In other words, the seed prospered in the thing which the Father sent it to do.

I began to look at the other ground in which the seed landed, and I realized that the seed that withered was like when the students would gladly try what I had instructed them to do when we were moving slowly on the mechanical steer, but then those good habits would wither when the heat of a fast-moving steer would be in their hands. This withered plant was just compost for more depth of root for the next time I told them. So, once again the ground was better for the seed having been there.

Finally, I began to see the way those who had come to my clinics with bad habits like the ones where the seed was choked with the cares of the world. They didn't want to give up the old ways for fear of looking bad. However, inevitably I would have them run a steer which would "burn" them if they used their bad technique, and then they would be ready to hear. Much like when you burn off a pasture of weeds if there is good seed in the ground the land will immediately start bursting forth with good grass out of the blackened soil. Once again, the ground was better for the seed having been there.

During this period, even though I wasn't fruitful, and I was often crapped on, withered and burned, my life was better for the seed having been there.

CHAPTER 4

The one place I seemed to be able to go to where I fit and where I felt alive was rodeo. I could attack the steer or the calf and even if I conquered it there were plenty more who hadn't been conquered. I wanted to be a world champion from the time I was about 8. So, I began to make most of my decisions based on the thought that I needed to do whatever it took to win a world title I would work really hard not because I liked to work but because I knew it took a lot of money to own horses and to get up and down the road. In short, rodeo became sort of a god to me. Whatever price it demanded I was ready to give. If rodeo said you don't need to date that girl she wants too much of your time, I would end it. If rodeo said I should be in the practice pen, that is where I would be. If rodeo said I should stay away from drugs I would stay away.

My dad was a good instructor. He was always for me, but he was also very hard. He would praise me when I did well but was sometimes very critical when I wasn't successful. He was and still is one of my heroes, so I would work as hard as he thought I should. Dad was usually good for a "good, but". He would praise what I did right but also point out where I could have done better. Growing up, this praise/criticism had the result of me feeling like I couldn't quite get there. I remember though the time when I felt the best about my preparation and the work, I was putting in. Dad was leaving to go to Ft. Worth for the winter run and he wasn't going to be home for a little over a month. We had just bought a new fresh set of 20 calves, and he told me when he returned home, the calves had to be roped out, (when cattle get practiced on for long periods they become obstinate and sour) or he wasn't going to get any more new ones. When he got back, they were the most roped out calves we had ever had. He was really proud of the work I had put in, and that felt great.

The work was beginning to pay off. I won the Kansas high school state title in calf roping my freshmen and junior years. I won the steer wrestling my junior year. I also won the average at the state finals all 4 years in the tie down and twice in the steer wrestling. I won the all-around at the state finals twice and the year end all-around my junior year. While the winning was great, what I remember the most were the losses. The toughest to get through happened my junior year. I qualified for the National High School Rodeo Finals in all three events (TD, SW, and TR). My partner missed in the team roping. My second steer fell the wrong way, and I couldn't get him to roll out. I made the short round and made a really good run. I was winning the average until the last guy went, and he moved me in the average by five tenths of a second. Then a month later, I qualified for the Little Britches National Finals in all three events again. This time I made the short round in both the calf roping and the steer wrestling. I drew a terrible steer in the final go-round, but I managed to throw him in 4.8 and was winning the title until the last steer wrestler moved ahead of me by 3 tenths of a second. My last event was the tie down roping. I was the last to compete in the final go, and I needed to be 9.3. The calf went a little left, but I still got him roped turned around and tied and I thought it was fast enough. However, when the announcer called out 9.4, I thought I was going to throw up. In the span of one month I had lost three national titles by a total of nine tenths of a second. Less than one second separated me from my goals and that was a tough pill to swallow.

I came home and swore I would never come up short again. I was wrong about that.

A few months later I watched my parent's marriage dissolve. This devastating experience, combined with the near misses in the rodeo arena from the previous summer, left me in a place by the time I entered college where my only focus was on becoming a World Champion.

While having a big goal and dream may keep you from making some mistakes, it will also keep you from even considering whether you are fulfilled. When anything, in my case rodeo, begins to be the sole focus of your life, you can become pretty myopic. My freshmen year of college I won second in the region in the calf roping and had made the finals in both events. My sophomore year, I began to focus on my steer wrestling to take it to the next level. That fall, I moved into a trailer house and, my roommate and three other guys began to have a routine. We would sleep in, do chores, then get the arena drug, and by noon or 1 o'clock we would be loading the steers to practice. We would usually be finished practicing by five or six then it would be dinner and a few beers, maybe watch a movie and be back in bed. This might seem like a pretty good college life, and it was certainly helping my steer wrestling; however, it was not very good for my grades. When the semester was over, I had not passed enough classes to be eligible to rodeo in the spring.

My father was livid, and I was crushed. When spring rolled around my routine changed. I went to class, then to work, then to the practice pen, and finally back to the trailer house which I was now alone in, have a frozen dinner and finally to bed. Unfortunately, without the college rodeos to look forward to I became even more depressed. I was depressed to the point I was in my living room, sitting on my broken futon, eating on my folding card table (which with a bed and dresser were all the furniture I owned), and I contemplated suicide. I looked around and didn't see a whole lot of value in me or in my surroundings. But, in that place as I sat there and ate my microwave meal, a thought came to me. The only thing I can do to make my current situation any better is to eat better.

The next day I went to the grocery store and bought a cookbook. I opened it and went shopping for the ingredients. It was odd, but this one change began to change my perspective. I saw that however bleak life may seem, there was a way through. I fell in love with cooking, and that simple act helped me back to a much healthier place.

> THE LORD IS NEAR TO THOSE WHO HAVE A BROKEN HEART,
> AND SAVES SUCH AS HAVE A CONTRITE SPIRIT. (PSALMS 34:18)

Good Pasture

... So he explained it to them: "I tell you the truth,
I am the gate for the sheep"

John 10:7

Many years later I was putting on a steer wrestling clinic, and we arrived at the arena to begin the third day to find the steers had escaped into a big pasture with a lot of trees and swamps and brambles. We rode out to gather them, and as we were riding through the dense undergrowth, I realized that wherever we went we continually crossed trails that were cut into the woods. I further realized that each of these trails lead eventually to the gate. Then, spiritually, I saw something new. Wherever we find ourselves Jesus has made a path from there to the Father. I am not saying that all roads lead to God, but what I am saying is whatever road you are on there is a path from there to the gate, and Jesus is the Gate of the sheep. *Jesus said to him, "I am the way, the truth, and the life. No one comes to the Father except through Me.*

I believe this verse whole-heartedly. Jesus is the only way to the Father, but there are infinitely many ways to Jesus. When I was in the brambles and broken-hearted after coming up short in a finals or failing a class, there was a path to the Gate. When things went well and I won a title, there was a path to the Gate. In the practice pen, there was a path to the gate. Riding my horse, there was a path to the gate. Wherever you are, look at your feet for a minute, and if you look closely enough you might just recognize there is a path crossing your path. Follow it and you might be surprised to find it will lead you to the Gate.

You see Jesus really did go before us. He has been everywhere you might venture and while He was there He marked out a trail for you to follow back to Him so that He can show you the way to the Father.

WHAT I LEARNED LATER

*"You shall have no other gods before Me. "You shall not make
for yourself a carved image—any likeness of anything that is in
heaven above, or that is in the earth beneath, or that is in the
water under the earth; you shall not bow down to them nor serve
them. For I, the LORD your God, am a jealous God, visiting the
iniquity of the fathers upon the children to the third and fourth
generations of those who hate Me ....*

Exodus 20:3-5

Many people are scared of God because of this verse expecting
fire to rain down from heaven when they put other things before
Him. Others read these verses and think of God as a killjoy setting
himself up against all of the other things in life that can bring
people joy or pleasure. Still, others can become incredibly religious
and feel that if a person doesn't avoid all of the abilities and skills
that come naturally to us then we are setting up idols for ourselves.

I believe it comes down to having a Father who loves us very
much and knows full well that if we choose to allow something in
our lives to become a god, we will end up being destroyed by the
very gods we have built. Rodeo had become my god. While rodeo
is a very good tool and I am extremely thankful that the Father
imprinted steer wrestling and calf roping on my DNA, rodeo
makes a really, really, bad god.

WHAT I ALSO LEARNED LATER

*If you then, being evil, know how to give good gifts to your
children, how much more will your Father who is in heaven
give good things to those who ask Him!*

Matt 7:11

Even when I was far from following Him, when my life was
for the most part set up in defiance of God, He still loved me.

31

Not only did He love me, but He gave me an incredible gift that has been with me throughout my life. The Father somehow knew me so intimately that He could see that the gift of cooking would help me regain some joy and hope. The cool thing is my Heavenly Papa loves all of His kids this way even when they don't follow Him. God gives incredible gifts to all of the people Jesus died for, and if I'm not mistaken, that is everyone. If you look in Chapter 12 of Romans, beginning in verse 6, Paul writes, *"In his grace, God has given us different gifts for doing certain things well. So if God has given you the ability to prophesy, speak out with as much faith as God has given you. If your gift is serving others, serve them well. If you are a teacher, teach well. If your gift is to encourage others, be encouraging. If it is giving, give generously. If God has given you leadership ability, take the responsibility seriously. And if you have a gift for showing kindness to others, do it gladly."* Many of those gifts are seen clearly in the lives of both believers and non-believers alike. So even before we call on the name of Jesus, His Daddy is giving good things to us.

CHAPTER 5

The summer before my junior and senior years of college I had the opportunity to amateur rodeo in Canada, and it was one of the best things I did for my rodeo life. I remembered how much I enjoyed rodeo, and yet it didn't have to totally consume me. I could work hard and still have fun doing it out of an internal passion instead of working as if I was trying to prove something to someone. My first year in Canada I lived in Swift Current, Saskatchewan. I worked during the week at a Ford dealership, and I was able to rodeo on the weekends. The experience was empowering. I was winning and learning, the people were great, and it wasn't nearly as hot as it was in Texas. That summer really reminded me of traveling with my mom and dad as a kid and of how much I enjoyed it.

The following summer I lived with Blain Wallburger and his family. Blaine lived 60 miles south of Elkwater, Alberta, 60 miles east of Manyberries, AB, 60 miles north of Havre, Montana, and 60 miles East of Cornet, Saskatchewan. It was truly in the middle of nowhere. The second day I was there Blaine and his family were going to drive into Medicine Hat to buy supplies, and they asked me if I wanted to go. I had come from the college National finals and had driven most of the previous day, so I said that I didn't and was going to ride my horses. I'm telling you the next time they went to town I was like a dog that jumps in an open car door and begs you to let him ride to town.

Staying with the Wallburger's was the first time I was able to truly be on my own. The previous year the place I stayed was a connection that my dad had made. I was in college and while I did pay for everything when I was at school, I could always drive the two hours north for a warm meal and a place to stay. Blaine was a connection I had made, and I had this opportunity not because I was Butch Myers' son. Furthermore, Blaine was a team roper, so I had to work out plans for my practice in the middle of nowhere.

He had one neighbor that lived about seven miles away and the Seville's were horse trainers. I talked to them and we struck a deal. I could rope as many calves as I wanted as long as I roped as many on their horses that they wanted trained. This was also the summer that I was able to put on my first two clinics that were just mine. My dad had begun putting on steer wrestling clinics before I was born. I loved helping with them, and I learned a ton as a student, an instructor, and later as an administrator. Canada was my first opportunity to try doing one on my own.

> DEAR BROTHERS AND SISTERS, WHEN TROUBLES OF ANY KIND COME YOUR WAY, CONSIDER IT AN OPPORTUNITY FOR GREAT JOY. FOR YOU KNOW THAT WHEN YOUR FAITH IS TESTED, YOUR ENDURANCE HAS A CHANCE TO GROW. SO LET IT GROW, FOR WHEN YOUR ENDURANCE IS FULLY DEVELOPED, YOU WILL BE PERFECT AND COMPLETE, NEEDING NOTHING. (JAMES 1:2-4)

As often happens with first attempts mine didn't go very well. The ground in Blaine's arena was mostly clay and it was fine when it was dry, but it rained on the Monday before the clinic and when we tried to work the mud it just kind of rolled up into balls. Those balls when they dried became little hard marbles. So, my students, which there were only five, had to learn to catch and throw steers on pretty much the worst surface possible to learn on.

My second attempt at a steer wrestling clinic went quite a bit better, although, it didn't look like it was going to. I held it at an indoor arena in Saskatoon. I was driving to the arena the morning we were to begin with a load of steers and equipment when I was pulled over by the RCMP (Canadian version of highway patrol). I only had a missing taillight, but the trailer I was pulling was borrowed, and he was not sure what a kid from Texas was doing it Saskatchewan with a trailer with Alberta tags. Fortunately, the owner of the arena happened by and vouched for me. After that shaky start, the clinic went really well, and I have had at least two schools a year every year since then.

These two summers were the perfect preparation for my rookie year in '92. I had won the college finals, won the amateur championship and finally learned how to win. These two summers let me enter the PRCA with $15,000 in the bank, confident of being able to survive on my own, and they reminded me that loving what you do goes a long way toward finding success.

GOOD PASTURE

However, the spiritual is not first, but the natural, and afterward the spiritual.
1 Corinthians 15:46

God's plan was to lead me to good pasture spiritually. However, He knew full well I wasn't ready to follow Him across the street let alone to the heights and depths He wanted to take me. My world was bigger than most, but it was still entirely too small to fit the life the Lord intended for me to live. So, God began by expanding my world in the natural. He took me to Canada where quite literally I could see farther. (In Saskatchewan you can see the curvature of the earth.) Then, when I was there, I was able to see it as an adventure which awakened in me a longing for more adventure. By making my natural life bigger I unknowingly opened the door to the potential for more than my natural life to be broadened. This was well before I was ready to follow the Good Shepherd, but it was work that the Father needed to do in me to prepare me for the day when I would follow Him.

WHAT I LEARNED LATER

The world has long wanted to make men tame, domesticated and quiet. Men either cave to this pressure and become docile shadows of the men they are to be, or they rebel against the feeling of control and become posers, phony, macho facades filled with trembling hearts. The devil certainly doesn't want men to realize the power they possess. He either convinces men to bottle that power and lock it away, or he bastardizes it and turns it into power over others.

Too often, men become either bullies or whimps. Some end up destroying the competition at work but find themselves scared to death to be the man in the other areas of their life. Or they become passive-aggressive complainers always whining about how the world has treated them bad but still afraid to do anything about it. They usually attempt to numb these feelings of inadequacy with one sedative or another. They sedate with sports, beer, women, anger, gambling... the list goes on and on. It all comes from believing the lie that they were supposed to be tame.

We were made in the image of a wild untamable God. The same one who made the Alps and the Amazon made us. Our big Brother took cord and braided a whip and ran off the mafia of the day. He walked on the sea during the storm.

> *The voice of the LORD echoes above the sea.*
> *The God of glory thunders.*
> *The LORD thunders over the mighty sea.*
> *The voice of the LORD is powerful;*
> *the voice of the LORD is majestic.*
> *The voice of the LORD splits the mighty cedars;*
> *the LORD shatters the cedars of Lebanon.*
> *He makes Lebanon's mountains skip like a calf;*
> *He makes Mount Hermon leap like a young wild ox.*
> *The voice of the LORD strikes with bolts of lightning.*
> *The voice of the LORD makes the barren wilderness quake;*
> *the LORD shakes the wilderness of Kadesh.*
> *The voice of the LORD twists mighty oaks*
> *and strips the forests bare.*
> *In his Temple everyone shouts, "Glory!"*
> *The LORD rules over the floodwaters.*
> *The LORD reigns as king forever.*
> *The LORD gives his people strength.*
> *The LORD blesses them with peace.*
>
> Psalms 29:3

The God we serve isn't a mamby-pamby kind of God. He is big and powerful. Jesus is, after all, the Lion of Judah!

And we are made in his image. When we will give God our lives fully He will release in us a powerful masculinity that will allow us to stand with courage in the face of tyranny. It will give us the steadfastness of purpose to be rocks which can stand unmoving as the sea breaks across them. Men can have the self-assurance to be gentle as lambs with the broken and as fierce as lions with those who would take advantage of the broken.

CHAPTER 6

It took me a while my rookie year in the PRCA to break the ice. Finally, I won second in the first round in the calf roping at Kissimmee, FL. Then, a week later, I won the steer wrestling and fourth in the calf roping at Tucson, AZ.

I was quickly learning that roping and steer wrestling were one thing but winning at the professional level was something else. For most of the first half of the year, I was struggling to find my groove. I traveled quite a bit up into Canada with Robbie Koontz, and I went with him through July before he went home. After Lovington, New Mexico I went to the Northwest and began to travel with Brad Goodrich, and I started riding Mike Sanders' steer wrestling horse. It was at about that time that I started winning consistently, and I was moving up the standings. The top 15 guys in each event qualify for the National Finals, and I was in the 16th spot with only two steers left to compete on. I knew I had to win something either at Glens Falls, NY or I had to place on my second steer at the Cow Palace (San Francisco). I rode a horse in NY that the guy said was easy to score, but the horse took the bits and I broke the barrier to win it which meant I was down to my last steer to make the NFR. So, we flew back to San Francisco, and I went up to see which steer I had drawn. I looked and saw that I had one of the worst steers on the herd. I walked through the convention hall and called my dad. I grumbled and complained to him for a few minutes about the horse in NY and the bad steer I had drawn. He listened patiently as I told him I needed to be about 4.5 on the steer to have a chance to make the finals. When I finished, he quietly said: "well I guess you need to throw this steer in 4.5 if you are going to make the finals." I was dumbfounded. I thought he would commiserate with me. I thought at least he would try to pump me up. I gathered myself and competed on the steer. I wasn't able to throw him fast enough, and I ended up missing the finals by less than $300.

To make matters worse my truck had broken down a week before in Washington, and I needed to fly to Seattle and drive home by myself. The entire trip (31 hours of driving) I reran almost every steer throughout the past year thinking of all the times where if I could have been a tenth of a second quicker, I could have won an extra $300. All of this negative thinking clearly had me distracted. I pulled over in Laramie, WY at about three in the morning, took care of my horses and slept until around seven. I woke up and filled the truck with diesel and got back on the road and drove for 2 and a half hours before seeing signs for Rock Springs, WY. That is right, I had been going the wrong way. So, I turned around in Rock Springs and had to fill up again when I got back to Laramie. It was a pretty miserable trip.

Although I had failed to make the National Finals I had won Rookie of the Year. I was invited to come to the NFR as the Rookie of the Year and to receive the saddle at the awards ceremony. I remember as I received the saddle I broke down in tears, and my family thought the tears were either because I was so happy or because I wanted to have made the finals. In actuality, the tears were because at that moment I realized that I had come really close to fulfilling my dreams and I was aware again of the huge gulf between me and any real joy or fulfillment. I was crying because I was scared. "What if winning a world championship didn't fill that void?"

The following year I was sitting seventh in the world standings and I tore my ACL in April ending my season. Then in '94, I ended up 16th again. These moments left me with an uneasy feeling. A feeling like something was missing, and I intuitively knew it wasn't moving up the standings one spot.

I had this thought in the fall of '94 that maybe this sense of dissatisfaction in my life was because I didn't have anyone to share my life with. At the end of December, I was preparing to trade my truck in. On the way home from removing my camper before heading to Oklahoma to trade it in, I wrecked it in Dallas. Two days later, instead of driving to Oklahoma to trade it in, I boarded a Southwest Airlines flight to Tulsa. This beautiful flight attendant recognized me, and after she told me who she was, I remembered her. I had known her as a small boy and later when I was in high school; she had dated a rodeo friend of mine. Candice was incredibly beautiful, and it was 30 minutes of angst trying to get the courage to ask for her number. Finally, just after landing I stammered something about wanting to catch up, and she gave me her phone number. Three days later, I was driving to the rodeo in Odessa, TX and I stopped at the Petro and called her from the payphone. It was 4:30 in the afternoon and after talking to her for about 15 minutes on the phone I said something like "well you've probably already had dinner but if not, would you like to come eat with me?" She laughed and said no she hadn't had dinner since it was only 4:30, and she would love to come eat with me. Since I had my horses in tow we couldn't go just anywhere, which meant we had our first date at the Petro truck-stop. Miraculously enough, she agreed to a second date. This time I had planned on taking her to West End in Dallas. We were meeting at Love Field airport and when we arrived it was pouring so instead of walking around in the rain we ended up talking in her car for about 2 hours. Finally, she suggested that we go to eat, so we left the parking lot in her car to run to Jack in the Box. As we go to walk in the door it dawned on me that my wallet was still in my truck back at the airport. So, my second date with Candice ended up being a trip to Jack in the Box with her paying the bill.

HE WHO FINDS A WIFE FINDS A GOOD THING, AND OBTAINS FAVOR FROM THE LORD. (PROVERBS 18:22)

Amazingly enough she kept seeing me, and by the end of six weeks, I knew I was in love. A month or so after that she knew the same. I proposed at the Reno Rodeo in June, and we were married in October, ten months after we reconnected. In the meantime, I qualified for my first NFR and we were headed to Las Vegas. I had a really good finals with a chance to win the world going into the 10th and final go-around. I needed to place two spots ahead of Ote Berry in the last go-round. Ote ran his steer right before me and moved to the lead of the round, so I knew as I rode into the box I could no longer win the title. I won third in the round and second for the World Championship. After it was over, I was pretty upset, and it probably seemed to most that I was upset because I didn't win. The truth was I was acutely aware that there was a hole inside bigger than any gold buckle could fill. Here I had a beautiful, intelligent, caring companion in Candice to share my life with, yet I still was aware of this void.

Good Pasture

For ever since the world was created, people have seen the earth and sky. Through everything God made, they can clearly see his invisible qualities—his eternal power and divine nature. So, they have no excuse for not knowing God.

Rom 1:20

One of the impediments that can keep us from following the Good Shepherd is our excuses. The Father wants us to be rid of them. When I called my dad before my final steer in 1992, I wanted him to feel sorry for me. After all, here I was at the end of my first season, and it looked like I was going to come up short. I didn't realize it at the time, but my dad's response was the most empowering and freeing thing he could say. In essence, he was telling me I wasn't a victim. Yes, the circumstances were bleak but to be using my excuse before I ran my steer was only to ensure my defeat. My dad chose to keep the possibility, however remote, that I might throw the steer down in 4.5 seconds alive. Dad was basically saying "I believe in you."

Our Good Shepherd does the same. He doesn't let us wallow in our victimhood, but Jesus says, "follow me." Paul reminds us we have been given the measure of faith, we have the mind of Christ, and that in all things we are more than conquerors. This doesn't mean that people aren't victimized. In fact, all of us have been victimized in one way or another by this world, but we are still given the free will to choose not to take on the identity of a victim. When we shake off these shackles, we can regain ourselves. Once we have released our victimhood and we regain ourselves, then we are ready to give our lives to the Good Shepherd and follow Him to good pasture.

WHAT I LEARNED LATER

Or do you despise the riches of His goodness, forbearance, and longsuffering, not knowing that the goodness of God leads you to repentance?
Rom 2:4

And Moses said, "Please, show me Your glory."
Then He said, "I will make all My goodness pass before you, and I will proclaim the name of the LORD before you. I will be gracious to whom I will be gracious, and I will have compassion on whom I will have compassion."
Ex 33:18-19

God is very sure of His goodness. He is certain that if we are honest with ourselves when exposed to His goodness we will turn to it. I feel like my whole life has been God knowing what I think I want. Then He brings me to the precipice of that goal or dream, lets me look over the gaping maw of that desire, and then He asks me a simple question each time. "Will this make you happy?" Each time the answer was no. During these first three years when Candice and I were together, we began to go to church. She would read her Bible, and I would try to read mine. I got baptized. I knew I was a Christian, but I hadn't given all my life over to God. I thought we just gave the bad stuff to Him, and He would help us to get rid of bad habits. At this point, I may have even said God is to be put first and He was. The thing is Jesus isn't just the Alpha, He is the Alpha and the Omega, the first and the last. He is above all things in all things and through all things In Him is all that ever existed or ever will exist. God doesn't just want our sin; He wants our life. He wants us to trust Him with all of it. Any part of our lives where we attempt to exclude Him end up empty because He is all substance and all sustenance. I was trying sub-consciously to love God with all of my heart except for the portion of my heart which belonged to rodeo, so that part remained empty.

What I needed was repentance. I, like most people, had a pretty negative view of this word. I thought it meant, "Stop sinning!" While this is the result of repentance, it isn't repentance. Some preachers teach repentance as turning from our sin. Once again this is a result of repentance, but it isn't repentance. The word in the Greek is *metanaio*. It comes from *meta* which means "after" and *naio* which means "to think." It literally means "to think after God," or to turn our minds to Jesus. Jesus Himself preached repentance. His goal wasn't to get our thoughts off of our sin, it was to get our thoughts onto Him. He trusted His goodness to lead us to repentance because when we see His goodness how can we help but think about Jesus?

Chapter 7

After we were married, Candice and I moved into our house in Van, Texas. The first Saturday we were there we had arrived home late Saturday night coming back from a rodeo. As we pulled into town, Candice asked me where we would go to church in the morning. I said maybe we should try several until we found a fit. We drove by several churches and looked at their marquee to see what time the services at each began. The Methodist church had the latest starting time and since it was so late when we arrived back home we decided to go there. We ended up staying there for the next 13 years. It is where I was baptized. It is where we both became very active in our local church body. This was the first time since those first months after my salvation that I had really given any attention to God. My wife was an incredible inspiration.

> HIS LORD SAID TO HIM, "WELL DONE, GOOD AND FAITHFUL SERVANT; YOU WERE FAITHFUL OVER A FEW THINGS, I WILL MAKE YOU RULER OVER MANY THINGS. ENTER INTO THE JOY OF YOUR LORD." (MATTHEW 25:21)

She displayed an authentic passion for God and His people that was infectious. We began to get faithful in going to church both at home and on the road. Candice is a singer and musician. At the time she was singing some in various venues when she wasn't flying for Southwest. It wasn't long before one of the preachers at the rodeos learned Candice could sing, and they began to ask her to sing a song or two at the rodeos. Once again, I found myself in a place to hear the Word of God and like those bleachers by the goat pens, it had the unmistakable ring of truth. By '97 Candice was singing quite a few times a month and she wanted to do her own stuff instead of just singing covers of other Christian artists. In '98 she began to gather the music and to write in preparation for producing her first record album.

In addition to beginning to attend church and to watching my wife worship and serve God, there was one more change that brought me a lot closer to God. In February, my son Layton was born. The instant love that bursts out of your chest when your baby is born is so powerful that it would be impossible for me to deny the pure unconditional love. He hadn't done anything to earn it, but my heart was flooded with this love. Additionally, there was a doubling of the love in my heart for Candice now she wasn't just my wife she was Layton's mom which gave me a whole new set of reasons to love her.

All of these things together brought me to a place where I knew I needed and wanted God in my life. I had heard Him knocking, and I had gladly let Him into the house, but I wasn't yet ready to give Him the keys. God put a man in my life at this time who kept quietly stoking the fire the Father had lit. Coy Huffman was and still is a cowboy preacher that goes to a lot of the rodeos. He sometimes does the church services; sometimes he just helps with some of the behind the scenes things that take place at the rodeos. He asked me if he could come do a church service at our steer wrestling clinic. Our clinics are always over Easter and Thanksgiving weekends and although we had never had a church service it seemed like something we should do. Coy came, helped at the clinic all weekend long, and then on Sunday my wife sang and Coy brought the message. It wasn't really the message that impacted me, it was the fact that he came without asking for anything. It was that he came for the entire weekend he didn't just preach on Sunday. Coy encouraged the kids who were nervous or scared, he pushed cattle, and he genuinely came to serve. Now, Coy at times can come off as a little odd to some of the cowboys, and I must admit I wasn't sure what to expect when I said he could come to our clinic and do a church service, but all my concern was extremely unfounded. I came to see that even his quirky moments were just his genuine love and following of Jesus.

Coy helped me in so many ways. He would challenge me to remember a scripture then test me to see if I had. I remember we left the short round at San Antonio and he said to me in a real matter of fact way "memorize the first Psalm before the slack at Tucson." The short round was over Sunday evening and Tucson's slack begins Tuesday morning and there is a pretty good drive in between. But because he said it as he did, something in me took it as a challenge. Sure enough, the first time I saw him Tuesday morning he began to quote the first Psalm and then broke off to see if I knew the rest. I recited the rest of the verse. The best part was that Coy knew I would have it memorized. This kind of confidence in a kid who wasn't sure he had what it takes to be a "good Christian" was powerful. I am so very thankful for Coy Huffman and the way he showed me the Father.

Another way in which God used my wife and her relationship with Jesus to draw me to Himself had to do with reading my Bible again. I had tried to get back into reading the Word, but I was struggling. Candice bought me a leather-bound Bible and a men's study Bible, but I was still struggling to engage in any sort of meaningful connection with what I was reading. One night, Candice and I were lying in bed and she was reading her Bible, as was her regular routine. I was attempting to read mine, but I just kept getting distracted or losing my place. I was sitting there wishing I could get into it like she did. About that time, I got this strange thought "I wonder if my name is in the Bible." My leather-bound Bible had a very small concordance in the back of it, so I looked. Low and behold there it was. Ecclesiastes 4:9 12: *Two people are better than one because together they have a good reward for their hard work. If one falls, the other can help his friend get up. But how tragic it is for the one who is all alone when he falls. There is no one to help him get up. Again, if two people lie down together, they can keep warm, but how can one person keep warm? Though one person may be overpowered by another, two people can resist one opponent. A triple-braided rope is not easily broken.*

That night was the first night where I felt sure that I had heard the Lord. I heard preachers say phrases like "hearing the voice of God" or "that still small voice" but for the very first time I was experiencing it for myself. All of a sudden I wanted to read my Bible. The words began to come alive to me, and as I read, I kept hearing and understanding what I was reading in a new and profound way.

Good Pasture

My sheep listen to my voice; I know them, and they follow me.
I give them eternal life, and they will never perish. No one can
snatch them away from me, for my Father has given them to me,
and he is more powerful than anyone else. No one can snatch
them from the Father's hand. The Father and I are one."
Yes, I am the gate. Those who come in through me will be saved.
*They will come and go freely and will find good **pastures**.*
John 10:27-30

I found that I hear the Good Shepherd's voice, which makes me His sheep. What's more, I can't be taken from His hands. Jesus had called me out of the sheep pen when I was twelve, and while I had hesitantly followed for a brief period of time, I had gone back into the pen. For sheep, the only reason to be in the sheep pen is to be sheared or slaughtered. Ironically, sheep are very comfortable being in the pen with the herd even though it isn't a good place for them to be. I, like most sheep, had preferred the comfort of the pen to leaving the herd to follow my Shepherd. I had stayed inside of the pen to become the baddest bulldogging sheep in the pen but had found very little satisfaction there. Now, I began to learn to hear the voice of my Shepherd and follow Him. Just like real sheep when we hear and follow, we begin to move away from some of the bleating, and we can hear Him better. At this point, I was willing to follow Jesus tentatively, but I wasn't ready to follow Him just anywhere. Narrow is the path and difficult is the way that leads to good pasture, and like many believers, I was willing to leave the pen, but I kind of just wanted to hang out outside of the gate. However, there isn't a more beaten down, muddy, barren place in any pasture than the area right around the gate. Like most Christians who only follow so far, I was left in that barren wasteland between the pen and the pasture. Interestingly enough, my Shepherd wasn't in a rush to make me follow Him. Jesus seemed to be pleased with me which in my mind seemed odd. He didn't even seem in any hurry for me to start producing. He seemed, in fact, to have no

48

plan or agenda at all. Jesus appeared to just want to hang out. As long as I kept looking back at the pen He wasn't really leading me to go anywhere. I always thought Jesus would be expecting me to achieve, to conquer. Most of the sermons I had heard had a lot of "going out into all of the world" language in them. Why was Jesus not "unhappy" with my half-heartedness?

WHAT I LEARNED LATER

But God has chosen the foolish things of the world to put to shame the wise, and God has chosen the weak things of the world to put to shame the things which are mighty; and the base things of the world and the things which are despised God has chosen, and the things which are not, to bring to nothing the things that are.
1 Corinthians 1:27-28

Coy Huffman has become for me the embodiment of this verse. He would do things which at times would ruffle the feathers of the Christians who thought they were really wise, but these very unusual methods bared fruit in that they were the very acts which the Father used to reach a lot of cowboys for the Kingdom. One time in particular Coy used a method that set all kinds of religious nerves on edge. He spoke to the students at one of my clinics from 2 Kings chapter 7 from when the Syrians heard the sound of the chariots and fled even though they had the people of Jerusalem completely on the verge of starvation. Then the lepers went to the Syrian camp only to find it empty. Coy played the "Who Let the Dogs Out" song as a thing the Syrians must have thought. It was meant to be silly. Still, some people grumbled, "what Coy is saying is borderline blasphemy." The interesting thing is though God used it. A bunch of the students that year gave their lives to God, and I saw Jesus use a foolish thing to shame the wise.

Chapter 8

In the spring of 1998, I went to the annual Duvall steer wrestling jackpot. At Duvall's, they have an event called Battle Royal. They invite the best ten steer wrestlers in the world and all ten run the same ten steers in a winner take all format. This event had some of the toughest guys in the world. I competed multiple years against guys like Todd Fox, Brad Gleason, Mike Smith, Steve Duhon, Ote Berry, Byron Walker, Rod Lyman, Frank Davis, Bill Pace, Victor Deck, Jim White and Herbert Theriot. These guys were the people I looked up to and admired. In 1998 I won by a wide margin and even threw eight of the steers faster than anyone else did. When I left the arena, Byron Walker, not a guy known for giving compliments, said to me "I think that is about the best anyone can bulldog." I guess I agreed with him and that was the beginning of a very rough couple of years. I say all of that not to extol my win but to illuminate the fact that an idea got into my head that day which started to work like a cancer that, had it gone unchecked, could have brought all kinds of destruction into my life.

> ... YES, ALL OF YOU BE SUBMISSIVE TO ONE ANOTHER, AND BE CLOTHED WITH HUMILITY, FOR "GOD RESISTS THE PROUD, BUT GIVES GRACE TO THE HUMBLE." (1 PETER 5:5)

The thought was "that might be the best I can steer wrestle." I had been teaching lots of clinics, I had been practicing with lots of really talented guys, and I had been winning on really bad steers. All of this opened the door for pride to slip in. In essence, I had put a ceiling on myself. By believing I had done my absolute level best I had sub-consciously prevented myself from doing any better. When you put a cap on your abilities, you may get close to that level, but you will always keep bumping up against that lid. Before long I could only see the negative in runs; I couldn't see the positive. So, I became increasingly grumpy about and angry with my steer wrestling. This became even more apparent in the practice pen.

I was now a professing believer and I didn't want my actions to be contrary to what I believed. However, this was never more difficult to live out than in the practice pen. I would have a steer escape, I would not make a good run, or I would make a mistake, then I would get mad and I would be cussing a blue streak. I didn't want to behave like this, and I tried all sorts of things to try to stop and now and then I would be able to contain it. Trying to contain this anger was reducing my energy and passion for my practice. I began to question if I would ever be able to attack the steers in front of me with the amount of aggression required to be effective. I began to question if I even wanted to keep steer wrestling.

One day in Malakoff, Texas we were about to practice, and while I was waiting for some other guys to show up, I started reading my Bible. I happened to be reading in Romans chapter 5 and these words leapt off of the page at me. *And not only that, but we also glory in tribulations, knowing that tribulation produces perseverance; and perseverance, character; and character, hope. Now hope does not disappoint.* I knew this was for me. I began to look at the steer that got away as a tribulation or trouble and now I was to glory in my troubles, for the tribulations would produce perseverance, the perseverance would produce character and the character would produce hope, and finally, hope would not disappoint. A month or so later, this went a little deeper when I heard James 1:2-8: *My brethren, count it all joy when you fall into various trials, knowing that the testing of your faith produces patience. But let patience have its perfect work, that you may be perfect and complete, lacking nothing. If any of you lacks wisdom, let him ask of God, who gives to all liberally and without reproach, and it will be given to him. But let him ask in faith, with no doubting, for he who doubts is like a wave of the sea driven and tossed by the wind. For let not that man suppose that he will receive anything from the Lord; he is a double-minded man, unstable in all his ways.*

I began to count it all joy, and even though I was still competing with this ceiling I had constructed for myself, I began to find some joy in chasing my dragons not just in slaying them.

At this same time, I made the decision to read my Bible from cover to cover. This and a few moments like my time in the practice pen began to change what I thought about the Bible- it no longer seemed like a storybook about things that had passed. I began to realize the value in the here and now. Consequently, my relationship with God was getting deeper, my steer wrestling was stagnant. I won more money than any other steer wrestler in the regular season, but when I got to the National Finals I broke the barrier in the first round to win the round and felt like I had blown it again. (Years later I watched the NFR again only to realize I was still very much in it) In '99 I continued to spiral in my steer wrestling though my walk with God was growing. I still thought I had to figure the steer wrestling out for myself. I watched film, practiced relentlessly, asked others for advice. Still, I was finding it hard to see what was happening in my steer wrestling. Finally, in the summer of 1999 and the following spring of 2000 three things happened that restored my love for the sport, humbled me, and caused me to become aware of the ceiling I had put on myself, and connected me to a deeper and more impactful purpose.

First, in July of 1999, Candice was about to give birth to our second son Holden. I ran my first steer in Cheyenne on Monday morning and drove home because we had scheduled for Candice to be induced the following morning. Of course, with a new child on the way and 14 hours of driving it was a good time for the Father to get my attention. I was in the area of eastern Colorado and the panhandle of Oklahoma and Texas with absolutely no radio stations available when I began to be overcome with this almost palpable sense of the presence of God with me in the cab of the pickup. Inside I felt like the Father was asking me to share my story. I didn't think my testimony was worth sharing, I didn't think anyone would want me to share, I didn't think I could stand up and give my testimony without stuttering and stammering, and finally, I didn't think it would be very helpful to those who might be willing to listen. However, the presence and atmosphere inside of that truck were so charged with God and His love that I found myself saying through tears, "God, I will do whatever you want."

Incidentally, a little over a month later Coy asked me for the first time if I would give my testimony at a church in Ellensburg, Washington where my wife was singing and Coy was preaching. I was petrified. I have this thing that sometimes happens to me where I can't think of the exact word I want to say in a conversation, and I get stuck at that point where I almost can't go on with the conversation. I was sure this was what would happen in front of the whole congregation with me stammering and losing my train of thought. As Candice sang, I was rifling through my Bible like it was a rolodex and I felt like I was a high school girl who just lost her prom date. Then just before Candice finished singing I ran across I Cor. 2:1-2: *And I, brethren, when I came to you, did not come with excellence of speech or of wisdom declaring to you the [a]testimony of God. For I determined not to know anything among you except Jesus Christ and Him crucified.*

I stood up, quoted the verse, spoke for another 10 minutes, had little or no idea what I said but after it was over, I somehow felt like what was in me was somehow released from me and those who were there seemed to have received something from it.

The second incident came early in 2000. A radio DJ teased a segment on the four P's of the successful life. I immediately began to wonder what the 4 p's were. Since it was a Christian station the first one seemed obvious. Prayer. Then I thought surely priorities, patience, and peace- those are some good "Christian" words. When the radio personality returned the first word was indeed prayer. I was one for one. Then he went to the second one which was "purpose" and my pride was skewered. His explanation of purpose broke a mindset that I had about priorities. I had heard somewhere, that you should put God first, your wife second, your kids third and your job fourth. The DJ confronted these priorities head-on. One of the first things he said was God doesn't just want to be first in your life. He wants to be the Alpha and the Omega, the first and the last, and everything in between. He then began to show how when we are loving our wives and kids or when we are doing our job well, we are worshipping our Father. He went on to say that living our lives by priorities has the ability to bind us which prevents us from following God the way He wants us to. Through some of his examples, I began to be reminded of patterns in my own life that showed how priorities had kept me from loving my wife and kids well, out of a sense that I "needed" to keep God first. I would get home from a rodeo trip and be annoyed when my kids wanted to play with their dad before I had finished my Bible study for the day. I realized that while it may be helpful to look back at my life and see if I had lived by the right priorities, in the moment, it was an unhealthy way to live life. This revelation was such a profound transformation in my mind.

This deeper understanding of purpose led me to the DJ's next p which was passion. If God was in all of life I could passionately pursue all that God had placed in my life. The next week when I was at the San Antonio Rodeo, I realized living in these religious shackles had stolen my joy. I prayed a simple prayer that morning in San Antonio. I asked God to restore my joy. When I prayed, I believed God would fulfill my request. What surprised me, though, was the speed at which He restored His joy to me. Before the day was over, I was seeing the things around me in a completely different way, I remembered all of the things I loved about what I do and the people I was blessed to be around. God had restored my passion not just for rodeo but for my wife, my kids, my horses, and my friends. It felt like when your horse has been wearing their blanket for several days in the winter because it is so cold. Then a day comes where the sun is shining, and you can take off their blanket and turn them out for a while. They run and buck and play like baby colts. That is how I felt that day. By the way, the final P was "people" and when the prayers, purpose and passion are in place it is easy to care for people.

Finally, a month or so later I was practicing and still having some difficulties with a certain kind of steer. I was counting it all joy when I was reminded of the next part of that verse, *"if any man lacks wisdom let him ask of the Father who gives to all liberally and without reproach."* I asked God to help me with my steer wrestling. In hindsight, this was a major moment because I was, in essence, releasing my self-reliance and submitting myself to God. At the time though, it felt like just asking another steer wrestler for advice. The amazing part was that He almost immediately answered my prayer. A couple of practices later I was stretching preparing to run some steers when I see in my mind's eye the placement of my legs when I kick out to begin the run. In my mind, I see my left leg move 6-8 inches to the left. As I see this, I understand the implications of what that would change in my run. I see how these six inches will make a wider circle which reduces the torque and allows the steer to turn more smoothly, relieving some of the pull on my right arm and making strong steers less strong while keeping weak steers from folding under the extra whip. The help to my steer wrestling was almost immediate but the bigger more impactful result of this answer to prayer was that I began to realize I could trust God with my steer wrestling. My heavenly Father was willing even to help me with such an earthly thing like bulldogging.

These three experiences with Jesus deepened and strengthened my relationship with the Father and radically changed my life over the years to come.

GOOD PASTURE

To him the gatekeeper opens. The sheep hear his voice, and he calls his own sheep by name and leads them out.

John 10:3

I am the door. If anyone enters by me, he will be saved and will go in and out and find pasture. The thief comes only to steal and kill and destroy. I came that they may have life and have it abundantly.

John 10:9-10

I love that the shepherd leads them in; He goes first. He doesn't chase the sheep or prod them along. The Way is completely voluntary. Jesus entered by the door and so became the door for us to walk away from the status quo. He knows His sheep. The Father knew this bulldogging sheep. Jesus knew where to find me, and when He called, He patiently waited until I was willing to follow. He spent the time when I was only comfortable hanging around by the gate to reveal Himself to me. Little by little I grew to trust Him more and more. Now I was ready to see where He might want to take me. Narrow is the path and difficult is the way, but Jesus is both the path and the way. Yes, it is difficult to leave comfort. Yes, it is scary to not know the destination. But why would I want easy? Most of the things in my life that are worthwhile or remarkable have been challenging and full of uncertainty. From my first competition, to riding a roller coaster, to making the first call to my future wife, to watching my children being born and growing, all of these were challenging but incredibly rewarding. Every day is full of difficulties, or maybe they are just full of life. Maybe that is why, in the garden, God gave men the Tree of Life from which we may eat freely.

What I Learned Later

He answered, "I heard you in the garden, and I was afraid because I was naked; so I hid."

Genesis 3:10

Men have been hiding behind one sort of fig leaf or another since the garden. Men hide behind money, accomplishments, girls, anger, stoicism, and a thousand other things like trying to be the best steer wrestler in the world. As if world championships or any other thing could cover for the weakness we experience. Our lives simply do not measure to the level of perfection and light that is in God. We have all missed perfection, and so we try to cover this gap. How could God love us in our current state? For that matter how could anyone love us? I mean the real us. So, we hide. Men have gotten really good at hiding, and we have been doing it for so long we almost (and I mean almost) believe the persona we have created is the real us. However, it is only in coming out from behind our masks that we find out who we are and who we can be.

CHAPTER 9

Before I go any further, I want to stop and back up for just a minute. I don't want to leave anyone with the impression that I just arrived or that I was a "self-made man". God brought some amazing people into my path. He brought some amazing mentors, some power-packed brothers, and some fathers in the faith who shaped, challenged, encouraged, and inspired me. God used each of these people and countless others to bring me to a place where I was ready and eager to follow my King.

FOR BY WISE COUNSEL YOU WILL WAGE YOUR OWN WAR, AND IN A MULTITUDE OF COUNSELORS THERE IS SAFETY. (PROVERBS 24:6)

I found three of these guys on the same weekend in November of 1999. Candice was attending a conference in OKC. It was a conference for people in ministry who were serving in the cowboy or western community. I went along to watch the kids, so she could attend the sessions. I went to some of the services when the boys were up to it, but at this time, I thought my only purpose in the Kingdom was to carry her heavy sound equipment, and I was more than happy with that arrangement. The three men who were leading the services and doing most of the speaking were Lynn Schaal, Andy Taylor, and Dave Morrison. Three very different Godly men who each taught me some valuable truths about God and His Kingdom. I learned from each of them, but more importantly, each showed me the Kingdom and the love of the Father by their actions. It started before we even left the conference. First, Andy Taylor in his genuine affable style talked about the Father. I don't remember the message, but what I remember is that when Andy spoke of the Father he was clearly speaking about someone he knew not just someone he knew about. Dave spoke about faith, and once again I can't remember the details but what I do remember is when Dave finished speaking my wife and I both thought Nate (Dave's son) was going stand up out of his wheelchair. Lynn spoke and again I don't remember all that He said but one phrase stuck. Lynn said, "our Church's motto is helping people so they can help others." He went on to say, "I am often told it doesn't sound very spiritual, I could make it sound spiritual by saying 'we minister to people so they can minister to others' because minister just means help." That statement went off in me like a bolt of pure electricity. I had never even considered that I could minister, but at that moment I realized I could help. Lynn, this man who was full of wisdom, had made taking part in the Father's redemptive plan simple, and that changed my life.

DAVE MORRISON

I didn't have the opportunity to spend a ton of time with Dave, but the times when I did it was impactful. Dave invited us to come to his place and stay when we went to Rapid City for the rodeo. He also came to Texas a couple of times and to our house once. Dave's faith is tangible. You can feel it when he enters a room. The message of faith has taken quite a beating and at times rightly so. Some have used it to advance their own agendas. But if you could see it in Dave and hear it in his gentle words, you too would see the awesome power and authority that rightly belongs to every believer. Dave showed me faith by taking me with him to feed his bucking horses and checking the mousetraps in the feed room. Spending time with him and watching the consistent way in which Dave always defaulted to an uncompromising trust in the Father and in His goodness was empowering. I came to know what faith looked like by watching Dave walk it out.

LYNN SCHAAL

The first time I got to know Lynn Schaal was at his home in Twin Falls, ID before his rodeo camp. I called him a week earlier to ask if it would be OK if I came and helped out with his camp. I had only met him briefly at the conference in OKC, yet when I came to his house for the instructor's dinner and hang out time, he welcomed me and asked me to give my testimony alongside people like Al Bach, Paul Tierney, and Lynn McKenzie. These were all World Champions and people who I respected, not only their prowess in the arena, but who I had watched walk out their faith with grace and excellence. Like Dave Morrison, Lynn brought me in and treated me like family. More than that, I wasn't some weird uncle that you put up with at family reunions; instead, I was a valuable member of the family who had something to share with the kids who had come to the camp to learn.

In the years to come, I found every opportunity I could find to spend time with Lynn and his amazing family. I would plan my rodeos to try to drive through Twin Falls and stay a day or two. Each time Lynn, Dorette, and his amazing daughters would feed me, both physically and spiritually. I have never been around anyone like Lynn Schaal who I learn from so consistently. It doesn't matter what the subject is; if I keep listening, I learn some nugget that surprises me, changes my thinking, and enriches my life.

Whether we were making a homemade team roping dummy, going golfing, or playing cards in his kitchen, Lynn would be imparting wisdom, encouraging me, or by his actions showing me the grace and peace that are only found in the joy of the Lord.

ANDY TAYLOR

What to say about AT?

Andy is the most salt of the earth man you will ever want to meet. From the start, Andy took my wife and me in as family. We would take different routes to go to rodeos so that we could stop in Sayre, OK to spend a day, a week, or an afternoon with Andy and Julie. We would come and help with Trinity's rodeo camp and if we had a few days off our kids would even choose to go to Andy's over Sea World.

The most life-changing message that we received from Andy is as He says it, "God is what He is, Father is who He is." Candice and I both began to really know what it meant to actually know God as not just a Father but as our Father. For me, I had an earthly father who was better than most. So, thinking of God in terms of Him being my Father wasn't hard. The difficulty was that God is so dynamically better than any earthly father that through my lens

I limited God. My dad was and is a great dad, but all dads come up short compared to how amazing our heavenly Dad is. I needed to learn that God will never leave, that His love is never predicated on how well I do, that the Father's voice is never condemning. Andy and all the people at Trinity Fellowship modeled that unflinching, unwavering, unending, unconditional love upon my family and me. Whether it was Darryl joking around with my boys or watching Buddy and Linnie serve with peace and joy, or experiencing the simple free worship, we had countless flesh on bone examples of God's love to experience in Sayre, Oklahoma.

My favorite thing though was sitting in Andy's office with my wife and Darryl Perry and just talking. We might start off talking about rodeo, our kids, or something trivial and before long we would be talking about the Father. Even now when I have a question about a scripture or about what I need to do in a specific circumstance, Andy always listens patiently then he responds with "Well what's the Lord telling you?" This is, of course, frustrating. I want him to just tell me what I should do but Andy doesn't. He walks with me to the answer, waits for me to find it on my own. This is an amazing picture to me of the Father, and incredibly empowering to have a man that I respect, trust that, given time, I will hear and be able to respond to the voice of God.

Ted and Linda Wiese

Ted and Linda had Linda's Cowboy Bistro that they took to the rodeos. They would set up their trailer and tent at the rodeos and feed the cowboys for free. Linda is an amazing cook and the food was incredible but more than that she and Ted loved on all of the cowboys who came to the rodeos. They would encourage them, walk with them when it went badly, and celebrate when it went great. It didn't matter if the cowboys were Christians or not they loved everyone the same. I have seen them give many a meal to hungover cowboys with no judgment or condemnation. Besides providing a home-cooked meal and a sense of home on the rodeo trail, they offered me something else. They offered me an opportunity to gather with other believers and both learn from them and also share with them the things I was beginning to understand about my Heavenly Father all while safely in the shelter of their wealth of knowledge and experience. We got to do this and eat some amazing pie.

DUDLEY HALL

I first met Dudley at Rob Farrell's Spring Gathering. The Gathering is an event held near the shores of the Brazos River in the middle of Palo Pinto County in territory once held by the Comanche. Rob invites men, mostly from the city, and they all rope, ride, sort cattle and play cowboy. It is great fun. I remember well the first time I heard Dudley Hall speak. It was a Sunday morning of the Gathering and we were sitting around the campfire with coffee in our hands. He quietly and patiently used a wooden cane to demonstrate the difference between God's love and man's love. The message was powerful but even more powerful than his words was his presence. At the time I couldn't have told you what it was I saw, just that I saw something unmistakable. Later when I read Dudley's book Grace Works I was able to put words to what I was seeing. In his book he talks about believer's learning to "sit down within themselves." This resting in the Father's grace is palpable in the life of Dudley Hall. Over the years the time I have spent with him in person and in his books has shown me the power of resting in the finished work of Jesus even as we put our hand to the plow.

On top of these fantastic mentors, fathers in the faith, and encouragers, God also brought me brothers. Men, some of whom had been walking with God longer than I, and others who were just beginning to follow. I learned from and was challenged by guys like Allen Bach who was always following after the Father and asking hard questions that made you want to dig deeper into your faith. Clay O'Brien Cooper with his quiet assurance of God's goodness is always patiently ready to lend an ear. Daniel Green stubbornly and persistently digs deeper. Stran Smith is energetically and unapologetically seeking the things of God. Cody Custer is steadfast and determined in his pursuit of Jesus. Ricky Green showed me how to simply and honestly trust God at His word.

These and many others encouraged, challenged, comforted, and at times corrected me in my faith.

In addition, God brought four brothers who were built for the adversity of walking the narrow and difficult Way with me.

TIM ROSS

When I first met Tim Ross, it was in Laughlin, NV, and initially, he kind of irritated me. A month before Laughlin, I heard a message about needing Pauls (mentors), Barnabuses (brothers for the journey), and Timothys (people to mentor). God was supplying me with some amazing "Pauls." I had Timothy's in the men God kept bringing me through my clinics and to travel with who I can encourage and teach. What I didn't have were any Barnabuses. Then a month or so later, we were in Laughlin, NV. I asked all of the guys I knew at the rodeo who were actively seeking the things of Christ to come hang out and we would get some pizza and try to connect and prepare to encourage each other and to actively try to bring others into the fold. I invited 25 or so guys only 12 showed up and Tim was not one of the guys I had invited. I don't remember what ruffled my feathers about Tim that first night. I do remember telling Candice about the evening, and after telling her who was there, she asked about Tim. I said I don't know he's sort of different. She responded with, "Maybe he is supposed to be your Barnabus," I literally thought, "I hope not." Then Tim and I got to spend some time together and I learned the immense value of having a brother who will speak to you honestly. Tim is a genuine lover of God, a brother who speaks with the heart and the insight of a prophet. Tim has often been a voice to help me follow after God.

CHARLIE KINGSBURY

Charlie Kingsbury was a guy who I had known for a long time. We had competed against each other from the early years when I was in Little Britches. He had always been a guy that I knew to be a follower of Jesus not by the words he spoke but by his actions. We had been friends, but it took me playing a joke on him when he asked me not to (and him getting upset at me) for our relationship to go to that deeper "brothers built for adversity" level. We were both in Twin Falls helping Lynn with his camp, and they asked me to do a game to warm up the crowd. Charlie had asked me again and again not to do anything to embarrass him, and I assured him I wouldn't, only to abuse his trust by pieing him in the face in the end. It took a bit for us to come back together, but when we did, we were fortunate enough to have a relationship that had withstood a test. Charlie has the most grace-filled view of God of anyone I know. He and his wife Lorissa are raising five unique, talented kids. During every season of my life since it has been incredibly helpful to have a brother like Charlie to talk to about being a good parent and husband and about what it takes to raise amazing kids.

Todd Pierce

I'm not sure I have ever argued more miles with any person in my life than with Todd Pierce. Todd and I are two guys climbing the same mountain from opposite sides. We would travel together to one rodeo or another, and we might stay up until 2:00 or 3:00 in the morning arguing about some point in scripture.

Usually, we would end the conversation with both of us a little closer to the summit. Some of the time he would show me my blind spots; others he would help me be even more certain of what I had learned about God. Either way, we always left with a stronger connection with each other and with the Father. I have never known anyone to go at life with as much gusto as Todd. I once told him that when I practice, I try to go at 90%, so when I am competing and adrenaline kicks in, it will push me to 100% and not over where I am overswinging. He looked at me like I was crazy like the mere thought of going anything other than flat out was unheard of in his mind. Todd taught me not with words but with actions how to follow and love the Father in a spirit of complete abandon. Todd loves people that way too, and that kind of passion is powerful and life changing.

Ty Bean

If you are someone who loves my kids and does that well, you are always going to be aces in my book.

Ty did and still does do that better than anyone I know. We would see Ty all around the country. He would be at a rodeo in Colorado one time then be at a camp in Idaho, then it would be at a conference in Oklahoma, but whenever you would see Ty, he would be spending time with my boys. We were in Lovington, NM in the middle of the summer, and it was hot and dusty, and the boys were playing in the dirt. Ty decided to go to town and buy them remote control cars then comes back and doesn't just give them the cars and walk away, he gets down in the dirt and plays with them while I competed in the rodeo.

Ty started a Cowboy Church in Hobbs, NM before it was a thing to start Cowboy Churches. He would invite my wife to sing with him at rodeo services or at the church in Hobbs. Ty has an incredible gift for understanding and applying the word, but more than that he also has the unique combination of humility and certainty. Ty trusted the Father in me and allowed me the space to voice the thoughts and ideas the Father was beginning to reveal to me. This empowered a young believer to say what he was thinking without worry that the much more mature brother was going to swat his simplemindedness down like a volleyball set too close to the net. Ty has the ability to woo people to the kingdom by living with such apparent joy that people want what he has.

Good Pasture

And when he brings out his own sheep, he goes before them; and the sheep follow him, for they know his voice. Yet they will by no means follow a stranger, but will flee from him, for they do not know the voice of strangers."

John 10:4-5

Like Andy Taylor says, if God would have wanted something other than a family, He would have called himself something other than Father. When we leave the sheep pen, we may leave it alone, but God immediately begins to get us in community with other like-minded sheep. He will connect us with sheep that the Holy Spirit has already led out to good pasture and who know how to walk with the herd to help each in the herd find their own piece of fresh ground. He also gets sheep that can walk beside each other and that will have each other's back when the wolves come around. Jesus definitely has a very specific and individual path for each of us, but that doesn't mean we were ever meant to walk that path alone. The togetherness Jesus paid for wasn't the togetherness of a team, or a company, or even the togetherness of a squad it is the hard-fought and life-giving unity of family. *But as many as received Him, to them He gave the right to become* **children of God***, to those who believe in His name.* If we are all His then we are all family. When believers humble themselves and walk in the harmony of kinship they can go anywhere the Head of the family takes them, and they can do anything the Head of the family asks them to do. I trusted Jesus enough to leave the safety of the pen, but He connected me with family to help me trust Him enough to follow down the narrow difficult path.

What I Learned Later

I continue to learn from these incredible men of God. They challenge me, encourage me, comfort me and teach me. The Father continues to bless me through the lives of these amazing men.

CHAPTER 10

2000 ended in a weird place for me. Both my brother Cash and I made the NFR. A month before the finals the news show 48 Hours asked to do an in-depth interview with us about rodeo. They were going to follow us at the finals with a camera crew. I thought, "Oh wow, this is cool." I had really started trusting God with my steer wrestling, and now I had an amazing opportunity to celebrate and tell the world about Jesus. I had made changes in my steer wrestling, I was surrounded by a great group of brothers who were strengthening my walk regularly, I was going to the NFR again and for the first time with my younger brother. It felt like everything was lining up to be **The Year**. With the camera crew in tow, we arrived in Vegas, ready to set the world on fire. To say it didn't go the way I hoped would be an understatement. For the first six rounds, I just didn't win much. I had a couple of steers land with a leg under them which made me longer than I needed to be. I drew a couple of steers that weren't very good but I was still solid in the average and as the seventh round began I thought I could still place in the last three rounds, win the average, and win a world title. I had a pretty good steer in the seventh round, so I told the reporter from 48 Hours "God has given me an opportunity, and it's time to get the job done." Well, I ended up breaking the barrier in the 7th round to win 2nd in the round. The 48 Hours team caught me right after it happened for an update and my response was "well my goal goes from being 3 days away to being 368 days away".

2001 began much the same way that 2000 ended. I felt prepared and ready. My horses were working great, and in the practice pen, I was consistently making the best runs of my life. My spiritual life was active, connected and vibrant. I was surrounded by good people to travel with and my connection with my wife and kids was the best it had ever been. Still, 2001 started with a whimper instead of a bang.

In early February of that year Candice, the boys and I were in Rapid City for the rodeo and staying with Dave Morrison and his family, when I felt like the Lord spoke to me. I felt like He was asking me to sell our place in Texas. I gingerly brought this idea up to Candice, and I was surprised to find she felt like God was telling her the same thing. When we got back from South Dakota, we cleaned up the place and put it on the market. We didn't know where we would live or what we would do, but we were both sure this was what God wanted.

At about this same time God began to be really clear with me that I was not going to rodeo for a living in 2002. I didn't know exactly what that meant. I wasn't sure if that meant I wouldn't ever rodeo again, or if I was going to do it on a much smaller scale. All I knew for sure was that He kept confirming that I wasn't going to rodeo for a living in 2002. When I accepted this, I began to find a peace about it. I realized I was OK with it, and more than that, I was even willing to quit earlier than that if the Lord wanted me to. That winter at the rodeos I won next to nothing. So, by the time the spring rolled around instead of having $15-$30 thousand won, I only had a paltry $5,000 won.

By April our finances were starting to get tight. The only thing that was keeping us afloat was Candice and her music. She had completed her second album by then and was being asked to sing at lots of churches, special events and concert venues. I was to the point of being ready to stay home. For whatever reason, I wasn't winning, and I wondered if it was time to just hang it up. Then we were asked to come to Jeff Copenhaver's church so that Candice could sing, and I could give the message. I talked about the confidence the believer should have even in tough times because we can read to the end of the Bible and, we win. I likened it to being a Buffalo Bills fan and seeing the 1993 playoff game playing on ESPN Classic. Seeing your team down 32 points at halftime to the Oilers doesn't depress you- it is exciting because you know how the game ends. Likewise, as believers when the world seems to be winning, we can just look forward to an exciting second half. In the middle of this message, I realized I should take my own medicine, so I said something along the lines of "currently I have less than $6000 won, but since I have confidence that I am going to make the NFR, I am looking forward to a fun and exciting second half of the season."

I would like to say it turned around after that, but it didn't. The year continued to be rough. In May, I was invited to go with a group of other cowboys into Angola prison to put on a rodeo for the inmates. Since it was just an exhibition we took really great steers from a stock contractor in east Texas. I threw a steer and roped a calf then I spoke to over 1000 inmates. Afterward, we shook their hands and gave them some toiletries as a way to encourage them and to make their incarceration a tiny bit more bearable. It was an impactful experience. A little over a month later during the Fourth of July rodeo run, which is one of the biggest weeks of the year in the world of rodeo, I was struggling. I arrived at Window Rock, AZ and went to look at the draw. I had drawn I chose to take to the prison rodeo in Angola a month earlier. I think, "All right, here it is! This year is about to turn around." I got a great start, but as I slid off my horse onto the steers back he jumped to the right and slung his head back and to the left sticking his left horn into my right ear and cranking my neck back and to the left. It nearly knocked me out. I was dazed, my ear is bleeding, and I could hardly move my neck, but I was entered in 6 more rodeos over the next 7 days. I wanted to come home, and I probably would have but my wife was the voice of reason and of God for me. She said to me, "If you come home, you are going to have to drive back by yourself and it does not sound like you are in any condition to drive for 15 hours." She also took a lot of weight onto herself and said, "Don't worry about the money. I have a lot of churches to go to this month and God will provide". Here was my sweet dear Candice taking our boys and driving around the country providing for our family, and she was encouraging me to stay in pursuit of my dreams.

By the time August rolled around, I had about lost all my confidence. I was still a long way out of the top 15 and beginning to worry. I saw my dad at the rodeo in Dodge City, and I asked him if he thought I should just go home since there wasn't much chance of still making the finals. He watched some of the videos we had of some of the runs I had made, and he told me he didn't think it looked like the problem was with my steer wrestling. He thought it just looked like a lot of different circumstances and that I should stay hooked.

Finally, the last time I questioned whether I was supposed to continue to stay out on the road competing happened in Pendleton, OR in September. The slack began that morning at eight and as I was getting ready I received a call from my wife saying something bad had happened in New York. It was September 11, 2001. At this point, everyone thought it was just pilot error or technical difficulties that caused the first plane to crash. I turned on the TV in our trailer and was able to get a TV station on about the time the second plane hit the South Tower of the World Trade Center. Time seemed to stand still. Then we heard a plane has crashed into the Pentagon. Horror officially set in. Meanwhile, the slack was continuing to take place in Pendleton. Guys were walking around in a daze trying to clear their heads before they competed. Everyone was glued to radios between runs. Then, the towers began to fall, and our questions turned to anger and fear. Cowboys and cowgirls, most of whom had families a long way from where they were in Oregon, were fearful for their families because no one knew the extent of the attack. We were all angry at the terrorists, but it was the sickening impotent anger that came from not being able to do anything about the situation. The United States airspace had been shut down so none of us could even go home any time soon. After the slack that day the phone lines finally became unjammed, and I was able to talk to my wife again. I told her I was coming home the next day. She wasn't even sure she really wanted me to come home yet because no one knew if something even worse was going to happen and the authorities were asking everyone to limit all forms of travel.

That night they had a church service in the bleachers of the Pendleton arena. The preacher was also reeling from the day's events. He began to speak, but I was hardly aware of what he was saying. All I could think about was trying to get home. Then I became really aware of what he was saying, and he was stuck. The speaker just kept repeating "sometimes you just have to continue, what I mean is you just got to continue, if you don't know what else to do you just have to continue …." He stayed stuck in a loop for what seemed like forever, then I realized it was God speaking to me. So, I said to the Father, "I get it. I will continue." The second I said that the preacher went on with the rest of his message. As soon as the service was over I called Candice again and told her what had happened. We both decided whatever else happened, for some reason, it appeared that I needed to finish the season.

I began to win a little more during the fall run. However, by the time Oklahoma City rolled around I was still outside of the top 25 with less than a month to go until the end of the season. It was in OKC that the Father spoke to me again in that still small voice. I was watching the slack and Curtis Cassidy rode in on his horse Willy. As Curtis competed on his steer, I thought his horse looks like he would work really well in Las Vegas at the National Finals. As soon as I thought that, I heard the Lord ask me "Would you like to ride him out there?" I pondered this and thought I would. Once again the Father asked me "Would you ask him (Curtis) if you could ride his horse in Vegas?" Of course, at this point in time, no one had ridden Willy in Vegas and not every horse works in that arena due to its very short dimensions. Still, I summoned up the nerve and I went to Curtis and said, "Curtis, I know it doesn't look like I have much of a chance of making the finals but if I do I think I would like to ride your horse out there." He said sure although I am sure he was thinking fat chance there are less than 10 rodeos left and I was nowhere near to qualifying. However, the last three weeks went incredibly well, and I won more than $21,000 and slid into the 14th place, incidentally, knocking Curtis out of the top 15. I had to call Curtis and his dad Greg and get them to agree to bring Willy to the finals. Still, I was certain the Father had asked me to go get on Willy for the NFR and I wasn't about to miss the chance especially after the way the Father helped me to finish the season.

God had me do one more thing differently that year leading up to the finals. In the past I would practice intensely, running everything, I could get my hands on. Instead, this year the Father had me run the same ten steers horseback on each of my practice days. The ten steers were all average strength, average size, and with no tricks. They were each a little different, but none of them were what I would call a real challenge steer. So, I prepared differently for the finals, and I went into Vegas with the very real thought that this would probably be my final NFR. I knew I wasn't going to rodeo for a living in 2002, and I assumed that I might not ever rodeo hard again. In the past, the thought of coming to the end without a world title would have put a ton of pressure on me, and my mindset would have been that I had to get it done this time or else. However, somewhere along the way, I realized if God formed me in mother's womb (Psalm 139), and if I was created in Jesus for good works and since those works were prepared beforehand (Ephesians 2:10), and if God knows the end from the beginning; then in my Father's eyes I was either already a World Champion or I never would be one. I still felt like this was part of who I was, but it no longer held sway over me.

I arrived in Vegas with very few people considering me to be a challenger to win the title that year which was fine with me. I was determined to run every steer like it was going to be my last time competing there. I was going to compete to the best of my ability, and I was going to give God all of the glory regardless of the outcome. Ed Knoche who was a columnist with the Dallas Morning News asked me early at the NFR if it was better to be at the NFR without the added pressure of being in a place to win the Championship. I remember thinking, "Well, of course, I can win the Championship, I'm here ain't I"

Historically the first three rounds hold the highest level of risk for all steer wrestlers and specifically for me. It is the first time through on the steers, and it is always difficult to guess how they will leave in such a small arena. For me personally, I had several major malfunctions in the first three rounds in previous years. So, Round 1 began with a solid run of 3.9 seconds which let me split 4th and 5th in the go-round. My second steer was supposed to be average speed and average on the ground. As I left the corner, I saw that he wasn't leaving like he was supposed to, so I pulled on the reins and got off just in time as the steer stopped and tried to jump out behind the hazing horse. I caught the steer and was able to keep him moving enough to throw him in 3.7 seconds to split the round with Bob Lummus. I came back the next night to be 3.6 seconds to split 3rd and 4th in the go-round. The first time through the pens of steers was complete, and I was right where I wanted to be, placing in all three rounds. In the fourth round, I talked my brother into switching off his horse onto Willy. Cash came out before me and threw his steer in 3.6 seconds. I went two guys later and we were tied at 3.6. With one guy left to go in the round, the producer had my brother and me mount up on the two victory lap horses. Chad Biesmeyer was last to go, and he went out and tied us both at 3.6, so I jumped off of one of the victory lap horses to give it to Chad. Then I decided to jump on the back of the horse Cash was riding and ride him double. Within two strides the horse was bucking, and my brother was showing out to the crowd and fanning him with his hat. I was laughing but being behind the cannel of the saddle is not where you want to be when a horse starts bucking. I jumped off when we got to the back end of the arena. Of course, everyone that night at the buckle ceremony and the next day kept asking me about getting bucked off the night before. This might have caused me to lose focus on the job in front of me by continually being asked about what was in the past. Thankfully the Father sent Al Bach with a message for me right before the 5th go-round began. Al came to me before the grand entry and said, "I think the Father wants me to tell you to 'keep your eyes focused on Jesus and not on what has happened in the past'". This message was perfectly sent and perfectly timed, it brought my focus back to where it was before the week had begun. All that was in front of me was making the best run on the steer I had that night with no concern for the past or for future results. Focus only on Jesus and the moment He had given me. I went out that night and was 3.3 to win the round.

The second half began with a steer that wasn't very good. Teddy Johnson had been 5.8 on him in round three. I threw him in 4.1 seconds and made one of the best runs I had made at the finals. I didn't place but making a really good run on a bad steer is a great feeling. In round seven I was 3.5 and won second in the round to my brother. Round 8 I had another steer that wasn't bad but was hard to throw fast. I ended up being 4.2 and the round stayed a little soft, and I ended up splitting 2nd, 3rd, and 4th.

Round 9 I was the first guy to go and I started it off with a 3.5. I was winning the go-round until the last guy went. Cash was last in the round and he threw his steer in 3.3 which dropped me to second in the round. I only write about this because when Cash moved me my 4-year-old son burst into tears because he thought that meant I wouldn't be the Champion. When my wife told me about this incident later that night it broke my heart that my young son had felt the tension and the weight of my previous attempts to the point that ending up second in this round could bring him to tears.

The night before the tenth round I didn't sleep very much. It wasn't nerves though; it was something different. I had realized even before making the finals this year that God was in every part of it. I had begun to realize that He had always been in every part of my life, but for the first time, I was aware of His life and love flooding into every corner of my world. I lay awake that night remembering a few other nights like this in the past. I remembered lying quietly in the hotel room during my freshman year in high school before the short round at the state finals. That night I was really concerned that I couldn't go to sleep, but at the same time enjoying a sense of awe and adventure that had seemed to be almost palpable to me. I remembered a similar feeling in another hotel room the night before the college finals short round. I remembered another hotel and another sleepless night before my wedding and yet another as my wife spent the night in labor with my first son. In each of these moments, I could now recognize that although I had thought it was just me and my thoughts those nights, there was, in fact, another with me in each of those rooms. Of course, now I knew who it was and the revelation of the pure intimate reality of a Savior who would never leave me or forsake me filled me with peace and thanksgiving. I was overwhelmed at His love and grace which Jesus was pouring into my heart and life. I couldn't wait for the final round to get there.

When the 10th round began as long as Bryan Fields didn't win the round and I was no-time I would win the title. I didn't even think about that, though, all I wanted was to run the steer I had. Everyone expected me to back off of the barrier, but that would have been thinking about what had already happened and not focusing on Jesus and the moment at hand. I got a good start, threw the steer in 4.0 and won 3rd in the round. I set the average record at 37.4 seconds and won the World Championship.

GOOD PASTURE

And they journeyed from Elim,
and all the congregation of the children of Israel
came to the Wilderness of Sin, which is between Elim and
Sinai, on the fifteenth day of the second month after they
departed from the land of Egypt. Then the whole congregation
of the children of Israel complained against Moses and Aaron
in the wilderness. And the children of Israel said to them,
"Oh, that we had died by the hand of the LORD in the
land of Egypt, when we sat by the pots of meat and when we
ate bread to the full! For you have brought us out into this
wilderness to kill this whole assembly with hunger."
Exodus 16:6ff

We shouldn't be surprised that between where we are and where the Lord is taking us there will be deserts. But somehow we are. We end up just like the Israelites. They had seen the amazing things that happened in the land of Egypt that made Pharaoh free them. They had seen the waters of the Red Sea part and all of this only 45 days before arriving in the desert. All the same, as soon as it got a little dry and their food began to run out they began to complain. I too had seen God do some amazing things in the last few years of my life and I told God I will do whatever He wanted. However, when the winning began to dry up I, just like the Israelites, began to complain and want to run home instead of continuing to follow. I am so thankful for the faithful friends, family, and fathers in the faith who kept me from turning back before I reached the extremely good pasture the Father had prepared for me. God was leading me to a pasture that was perfectly suited for who I am. When we have spent too much time in or around the pen(world), we can begin to be small in our own eyes. Pretty tame and fluffy.

The thing is we were made for a different terrain than the soft, tame land where we are comfortable. We were born for bigger, more rugged, less safe pastures. We were born for higher ground.

The challenge of following the Father awakens some deeper sturdier part of us that does not run from the hard or the difficult but that begins to see the challenges as a great vantage point to witness the greatness of God on display.

If we will continue to trust the Father and keep following Him, He will keep meeting all of our needs along the way even if it means bringing quail in the evening and manna in the morning. Exodus 16:13-15: *So it was that quail came up at evening and covered the camp, and in the morning the dew lay all around the camp. And when the layer of dew lifted, there, on the surface of the wilderness, was a small round substance, as fine as frost on the ground. So when the children of Israel saw it, they said to one another, "What is it?" For they did not know what it was.*(Manna)

God can even take you from 23rd in the standings on Oct 23rd with one week left in the season, to 14th when the regular season was over, to first after the finals.

Trust the Father! He has a good pasture for you also.

Chapter 11

I was asked numerous times after winning the Championship if I had come down from winning the title, and the answer was always no. It was an amazing thing to experience, but it wasn't the pinnacle.

I knew the Father had said I wasn't going to rodeo for a living in 2002, but I didn't know what that really meant. However, it became a little clearer on the trip home from the NFR. On the way home a pastor from Valentine, NE called and asked if Candice and I could come and lead a community-wide service to be held in January. We were trying to decide whether to say yes when Dave Morrison called and asked if when I was up for the Rapid City rodeo, could I come to speak at four services? We realized the event in Valentine was perfectly timed for the trip up to Rapid City. The more we prayed about it the more it became apparent the Father wasn't asking me to quit completely but instead to enter and go to the rodeos where He provided an opportunity to share my testimony of His goodness.

Another thing happened in early January which made God's will more evident to Candice and me. We had faithfully had our house on the market for nearly a year with remarkably few lookers and no one even kind of interested in putting down an offer. We had lowered the price on the place 2 or 3 times all to no avail. In early January Candice and I were in separate places, and God showed both of us individually why we had put the place on the market. I was driving to Tyler listening to a Christian station when the DJ offered two tickets for a local concert for anyone who knew the name of the place where Abraham had offered up Isaac. I just happened to know the answer to his question. My wife has a song on one of her CDs called "Beyond the Temporary" and in the song she sings "and Jehovah Jireh was his name." I was listening intently for the answer to be given over the radio. At the next break, a caller replied Jehovah Jireh. The DJ replied," that is correct. Do you know what Jehovah Jireh means?" The caller said, "the Lord will provide." In that instant, I knew that we were supposed to take the house off the market. When I told Candice later that day, she had had a similar experience and we both agreed God had asked us to put our house on the altar, so we would know that we had truly surrendered our lives to Him. Like all sacrifices to the one true God, there is nothing given up to Him that He doesn't provide much more. One of the coolest by-products of this was we now loved where we lived way more than we had when we were asked to lay it down.

Another cool moment happened in April of that year. We were invited back to Jeff Copenhaver's church, and before I got up to speak, Jeff said he had a surprise for me. He then proceeded to play back my message from the previous year especially the part where I said, "currently I have less than $6000 won but since I have confidence that I am going to make the NFR I am looking forward to a fun and exciting second half of the season." It surprised me to some extent because I didn't remember feeling all that confident. But the Lord has a way of taking even the smallest seed of faith and producing all kinds of life with it.

The best moment for me, though, happened in California. I went to Red Bluff, CA for the rodeo and to speak at the Cottonwood Cowboy Church just north of Red Bluff. At one point during the message, I said most cowboys won't give their whole lives to Jesus because they are afraid He will send them to Africa. I made a joke or two about what God might want to do with a bunch of cowboys in Africa, and then seriously remarked that if He wanted to send you to Africa, you would first probably have the desire in your heart. The next morning, I was talking to my wife and she said to me "so do you want to go to Africa?" The crazy thing is I did want to go. I told her that I did want to go, and she told me the mission trip would cost us $3000 with $300 due now as a deposit. I was not rodeoing the same way, so we didn't have a lot of extra income. As we talked, I opened my Bible. Now, the night before after the service, as I was talking to some young men who had been battling some addictions, this man came up to me and handed me a folded-up note and said I could read it later. As I spoke to my wife about where we were going to come up with $300 let alone the $3000, I opened the note and inside were three one-hundred-dollar bills. It was such a cool moment with the Father to see Him Speak through me, supply my needs, and reveal to me my own heart.

The trip to Africa was incredibly impactful. We flew to Entebbe, Uganda and rode a bus to Mbale, Uganda where we spent three weeks speaking to over 7000 kids in schools during the day, then speaking at conferences each afternoon with pastors from all over Uganda, Kenya and even Tanzania. Each evening we would be at big crusade style events with 1000-2000 people mostly standing or sitting all coming from miles around to hear the Word of God. They had no idea what a cowboy was other than John Wayne and although I brought some ropes to try to make a connection it was mostly lost on them.

> BUT SEEK FIRST THE KINGDOM OF GOD AND HIS RIGHTEOUSNESS, AND ALL THESE THINGS SHALL BE ADDED TO YOU. (MATTHEW 6:33)

At one school I finally cracked up at myself. I had my rope out trying to explain what I do before talking to them about Jesus. The school had a huge hole in the side of the building where a bomb had caved in the corner of the structure and through the hole, I could see a cow that was tied up in the yard beside the school. I walked out through the hole in the wall and I roped the cow, who barely looked up from chewing its cud. The kids looked at me like "wow that was really tough". On the other hand, when we would tell them about the Kingdom of God they would be hanging on every word as if it was the bread of life itself (which it is). When we spoke at the schools with older kids, they would be split into two groups. I asked about this and they said one group was Muslim and the other Christian. However, to them, Christian meant only non-Muslim and within the Christian group was the group they called born-agains. At times when a speaker was sharing the Word with these older groups of kids, you would watch a young person quietly stand up from the Muslim group, walk over, and sit with the Christians. They would do this even though that very act meant they would be expelled from their families. The amount of courage that took was awe-inspiring.

In 2002 I went to 30 rodeos. Won nearly $40,000. I spoke to over 30,000 people in churches and services on two continents. Taught 7 clinics and camps. No, the World Championship was not the peak.

GOOD PASTURE

I am the door. If anyone enters by Me, he will be saved, and will go in and out and find pasture. The thief does not come except to steal, and to kill, and to destroy. I have come that they may have life, and that they may have it more abundantly.
John 10:9-10

The Father leads us out to new pasture but not to get fat and to spend our life chasing after material things. God knows us too well to think that kind of life would be big enough for children of the Most High God. No, He leads us out to find the kind of sheep we really are then He brings us back to the sheep pen so that other sheep will see in us what it looks like to live free and purposeful lives. The same way believers like Al Bach, Coy Huffman, Andy Taylor, Lynn Schaal, and Rickey Green came back to the pen to show me that following the Lord was the way to life. He brought me back to the pen with a story to tell of His goodness and grace.

The same way we can become comfortable in the sheep pen we can also become comfortable on the mountain. After all, when you get used to the peace of the good pasture, it is hard to even think about going back into the tumult. But imagine if Jesus had fallen for that. He had some amazing times with the Father in perfect communion with His Dad. He could have said yes to Peter when Peter asked Him if Jesus wanted John to make some huts for Jesus, Moses, and Elijah. Luke 9:28-36: *Now it came to pass, about eight days after these sayings, that He took Peter, John, and James and went up on the mountain to pray. As He prayed, the appearance of His face was altered, and His robe became white and glistening. And behold, two men talked with Him, who were Moses and Elijah, who appeared in glory and spoke of His decease which He was about to accomplish at Jerusalem. But Peter and those with him were heavy with sleep; and when they were fully awake, they saw His glory and the two men who stood with Him. Then it happened, as they were parting from Him, that Peter said to Jesus, "Master, it is good for us to be here; and let us make three tabernacles: one for You, one for Moses, and one for Elijah"—not knowing what he said. While he was saying this, a cloud came and overshadowed them; and they were fearful as they entered the cloud. And a voice came out of the cloud, saying, "This is My beloved Son. Hear Him!" When the voice had ceased, Jesus was found alone. But they kept quiet, and told no one in those days any of the things they had seen.*

When His children are filled with His glory and life, He wants them active and engaged in this life. Why? Because, He loves all His kids the same, and He wants us to have that same love. That is why staying on the mountain gets so old so quickly. We have a deep, deep desire for purpose, and that purpose although carried out many, many ways is basically the purpose of gathering our brothers and sisters to our Father at the leading of our big brother Jesus.

Then the LORD told him, "Reach out and grab its tail."
So Moses reached out and grabbed it, and it turned back into
a shepherd's staff in his hand.

Exodus 4:4

Moses saw the burning bush and the Lord asked him to go back to Egypt so God could use him to set the Israelites free. He was afraid they wouldn't listen to him, so God asked Moses to throw down his shepherd's staff. Now a shepherd's staff is the tool of the shepherd. It is quite useful in sorting, doctoring and keeping sheep. God asked Moses to lay down shepherding which was Moses' life at the time. Then the miracle—the staff became a snake, and if that wasn't enough, God then asked him to pick it back up. In other words, Moses had to reach down and grab the tail of the snake. I don't think Moses ever looked at that staff the same way again. All of a sudden this ordinary, earthly tool had the power of God in it. By simply trusting the Lord and laying it down, Moses saw the power of God. This is exactly what happened with my steer wrestling after the 2001 and 2002 seasons. I laid my steer wrestling down and God had shown His power through it. I could never look at my steer wrestling the same way. I now saw bulldogging as something that the Father could fill with His power and a tool He could use to change people's lives.

What are you holding onto that the Father wants you to lay down? I am not talking about sin or bad habits but what are the "good" tools that God has put into your life which He may want you to lay down so you can see what He can do with them.

What I learned later

Glory is a word used a lot in the bible but for a long time, I didn't have a good idea what it meant. In the Old Testament the Hebrew word is "*kavod*" and the New Testament Greek word is "*doxa.*" The word means weight or substance. The opposite is emptiness or vanity. Glory is the reality or the substance of God. The idea is that anything apart from God is empty, and God brings glory or substance to our days, our lives, our everything. John 17:1: Jesus spoke these words, lifted up His eyes to heaven, and said: *"Father, the hour has come. Glorify Your Son, that Your Son also may glorify You."* Jesus is asking to make His life full of weight and substance, to make it matter, or to be impactful. Jesus then takes the Glory given to Him by His Father and gives it to us. John 17:22: *And the glory which You gave Me I have given them, that they may be one just as We are one."* When we live out our life in Him, our life can have weight to it. Our lives can matter, they can make a difference. All we need to make them more weighty is to remove more of ourselves from them to allow more space for our glorious King.

Chapter 12

There things made 2003 extremely hard.

First: I was back to rodeoing for a living, and I went back to winning, but for the first time I wasn't able to take my family with me for a large portion of the season. My oldest son Layton was now in school and every time I had to leave to go to a rodeo they had to stay home. It felt a little bit like being split in half. He was beginning to play soccer and T-ball and so more and more often I had to choose between making a living or staying home and seeing my boys grow up. The one good thing about rodeo was that when I was home, I could be completely home. I could quite literally be with my family for 24 hours on the days when the boys didn't have school. This was a blessing, but it made being gone all the worse. I was starting to think of what I could or would do when the time came to quit steer wrestling for a living. I knew the time would come to do something else, and I kept looking to the Father to tell me when that would be. Candice and I were pretty sure it wasn't yet time to move on.

Second: Part of looking to the future made me wonder what kind of business I could run that would work with what I do and help provide a steady income for my family. In December of 2002, my dad started talking to me about building a Christmas light park. It would be a multi-acre park where people would be charged to drive through and see the lights. We decided to go in as partners and bought a piece of land on I-20 about 45 minutes east of Dallas. It is a lot of work to build a light park from scratch. We had to clear brush and trees, build roads, drop four different transformers, wire thousands of outlets, and a million other details. All of this in between trying to rodeo and be a good dad.

Finally: Both of these things made the year more difficult, but the worst part of 2003 was still to come. Candice was pregnant again, and we were certain it was going to be a girl. I was giddy with excitement. I love my boys, but I also really wanted a little "daddy's girl." We even had a name picked out- Zoe, which means the God kind of life. In the middle of June, Candice went in for a regular check-up with her doctor. Up to this point, everything had seemed normal. But something wasn't right. The doctor was having trouble finding the heartbeat with the doppler so he sent us over to get a sonogram. We began to pray and contacted some of our closest Christian friends to ask them to pray too. When we arrived at the sonogram place, I felt like I heard God say a scripture to me, so I grabbed my Bible and I looked it up. It was John 1:4: *Life was in Him, and that life was the light of men. That light shines in the darkness, yet the darkness did not overcome it.*

Another translation says "the darkness couldn't extinguish it." We felt like it was an answer to prayer. We went into the sonogram ready to hear them say everything was going to be OK. When the images began to appear on the screen are hearts began to fall. We left there with the doctor and nurses looking very solemnly at us and preparing us to schedule a procedure to take the baby. Still, we doggedly held onto belief. The Father had said to us that the Light shines into the darkness and the darkness did not, could not overcome it. We went to the hospital two days later for the surgery and we asked the doctor to get a doppler one more time to listen and see if there was a heartbeat. We just couldn't believe that our sweet baby Zoe was not going to be born as healthy as our two boys. Finally, with no heartbeat to find, my wife was wheeled into the operating room, and I was sent to the waiting room. The small windowless room was full of people, and all I wanted was to be alone. I wanted to cry, I wanted to scream at God. "How could this be happening?" I reread John chapter one. How could I have missed the voice of God by so wide a margin? I felt alone and I felt guilty for feeling that way after all my wife was the one going through a horrible procedure. What seemed like an eternity later, a nurse came into the waiting room and asked me to come to the recovery room. Candice was starting to awaken from anesthesia. When I walked into the room, the most amazing thing was taking place. My wife, while still partially coming up from being under, began to speak about how good God was. She began to speak incredible words of blessing over the nurses who were in the room. Her entire countenance was full of joy and life. I began to cry. Both nurses had tears streaming down their faces. For nearly 10 minutes she spoke with grace and power, it was as if her whole body was full of light. Then I realized the Light shines in the darkness and the darkness cannot overcome it.

The moment was powerful and definitely helped us in the weeks and months to come but those months were by no means easy. We had lost a child, but the world kept turning. We still had to care for our boys. We still had to make a living. I still had a new business that was barely underway. My heart felt like it just kept breaking, but I also felt like I couldn't let it show. I had to be there for Candice, and I couldn't be there for her if I was falling apart. Rodeo became kind of a blur. Working at the light park with my dad became almost untenable. Finally, one day about 50 feet up in the air working on the entrance sign I came to a breaking point. My dad was upset that I hadn't been putting in enough time on the park and I kind of snapped. I ended up hollering at my dad saying I shouldn't be there at all I should be home with my wife. I told him it was barely two weeks since we had lost a child, and if he didn't understand this, then we needed to end the partnership right then.

> SO WHEN THIS CORRUPTIBLE HAS PUT ON INCORRUPTION, AND THIS MORTAL HAS PUT ON IMMORTALITY, THEN SHALL BE BROUGHT TO PASS THE SAYING THAT IS WRITTEN: "DEATH IS SWALLOWED UP IN VICTORY." "O DEATH, WHERE IS YOUR STING? O HADES, WHERE IS YOUR VICTORY?" (1 CORINTHIANS 15:54-55)

For a son who had pretty much idolized his father for most of his life, this was a pretty wide departure. Something began to break loose though during those days, weeks, and months. I began to get free from a need for my dad's approval. I began to see him as a man not just as my dad or as some sort of idol. Seeing him as more human and less Superman did two very opposite things. For one I began to see him as a human with flaws, while at the same time being able to forgive him for them. He could be a man who was worthy of my respect. The admiration was now a matter of choice and could be seasoned with grace.

The road back to health and peace wasn't easy or short for Candice and me. But God kept restoring things a little at a time. We spent a lot of time with Andy in Sayre, OK. We also went to Twin Falls to be with Lynn Schaal for his camp. Lynn didn't ask Candice to sing but let her know if she felt like it, she could. I didn't think she would choose to sing but she did, and through tears, I could begin to see the light again.

The year in rodeo was pretty much a blur. In fact, I can't remember a single detail from the rodeo season. Evidently, it went fairly well. I ended up making the finals in less than 55 rodeos. The finals were kind of a blur as well. The Christmas light park opened and was successful for its first year. Mainly I just couldn't wait for 2003 to get over with.

In January of 2004 I asked Dad to buy me out of the light park. He did and our relationship was better for it. Soon after, Candice was pregnant again—due during the NFR in December—and it felt like we were back on the path following our Savior.

In May and June, I once again took a month off of rodeo to tithe back and help with three rodeo Bible camps. Andy Taylor's in Sayre, OK, Randy Weaver's camp in Conroe, TX and Lynn Schaal's in Twin Falls, ID. Between Randy's camp and Lynn's, I told my wife "I really wish we could put a camp like this on where we live. Candice said, "Don't even think about it. We don't have the infrastructure or the help to try to pull something like this off in Van." The next week I was in Twin Falls. I call home and Candice said to me "Do you still think you want to put on a camp in Van?" A few weeks earlier she had been invited to sing at a big FCA event in Tyler, TX. The main speaker's plane was delayed and so they asked her to stretch and what began as a 10-minute set became 30 minutes and her giving a message while waiting for the speaker. After the event, a lady asked her if she would come and sing at the all-staff meeting for a ministry called Sky Ranch. Sky Ranch was located just outside of Van, and we had seen the signs for it many, many times, but we never knew what it was or even exactly where it was. Candice sang at their all-staff event a few weeks later, and after it was over, while they asked questions about our ministry, she told them that I was in Idaho helping with a rodeo camp. Sky Ranch is a summer camp among other things, yet they had never even heard of such a thing as a rodeo camp. They were intrigued and invited us both back out to talk to them about what we do. Candice and I came out a few months later, and we met with the CEO and several of the leadership staff. The meeting was scheduled for an hour, but two and a half hours later Candice and I walked to the car and we looked at each other and said, "I think we work there now."

By November we did work there. They hired me on a consultant basis with the goal to have one rodeo camp the following summer. My first day working at Sky my boss asked the guy who currently ran the rest of the horse program to give me the tour of the place. He drove to the main gate, switched off the pickup, turned in the seat to look at me and said, "This is nothing against you, but if they are going hire you I am quitting." I tried to explain I wasn't being placed over him; I was just coming with the sole purpose of beginning a rodeo camp program. It didn't matter what I said, the die had been cast and he quit that same day. My boss was a great guy named Terry Binder. He brought me in his office and said, "well cowboy do you think you can run the whole department?" The department consisted of 70 head of horses—only 30 of which you could ride and less that you could put guests on. There were four full-time staff and three part-timers who loved their old boss and were pretty sure I was the enemy, and that I was the reason their old boss had lost his job. All this took place in the first two weeks in November. My wife was due the first of December and the Finals started on the third.

Our annual steer wrestling clinic was the weekend following Thanksgiving. After it finished on that Sunday we packed our bags and prepared to go to the hospital Tuesday morning. Candice was scheduled to be induced at 6 am. Everything went smoothly until the very end. By the middle of that afternoon, our daughter was being delivered. Praise God for an amazing old army doctor that had delivered nearly 10,000 babies because as our baby began to emerge the doctor told Candice to stop pushing, and I watched as he threaded his fingers under my daughter's chin and beneath the umbilical cord which was wrapped around her neck twice. He deftly slipped it over her head, and she was born safely. With a huge sigh of relief, I looked down at my beautiful baby girl. Things had come full circle and while we wouldn't get to meet Zoe until we went to heaven, we now had Tierney Faith, and faith is the substance of things hoped for. That night I held her all night. She slept on my chest, and she kept sighing. It was incredibly sweet. The sad part for me was I had to leave the following morning to fly to Las Vegas for the NFR which started on Friday.

That NFR was a strange one for me. It was the first and only NFR where my family didn't attend. My brother didn't qualify, and my dad didn't come either. I had a room just a few blocks from the Thomas and Mack coliseum and I spent most of my time either in the room or taking care of my horse. I had a good finals placing in six rounds and ended with winning the tenth round and finishing with a 44.0 average on 10 head. I flew out hours after the final go-around to get home to see my beautiful daughter and the rest of my amazing family. While it didn't have the spectacular ending that 2001 did, it was still very satisfying to me. It felt very similar in the closeness that I had with the Father and the connection I had with my family and my friends. I was in a place of peace with the ability to do what I loved while not being controlled by the outcome.

GOOD PASTURE

These things I have spoken to you,
that in Me you may have peace. In the world
you will have tribulation; but be of good cheer,
I have overcome the world.

John 16:33

The Father was leading us out again to a new "good pasture." He was going before us, but he never promised us a trouble-free life. God knows that from the fall of man this world has suffered the brokenness inflicted upon it by sin. Things are no longer the way they were made to be in the garden. Man, in Adam, had committed high treason by submitting his will to God's arch-enemy. Man was given dominion or rule over the entire earth. Adam and Eve were put in charge and given a life free from shame, free from guilt, and free from pain. They were given all the plants that bore food and fruit to eat. The only thing they were forbidden from doing was to eat from the tree of the knowledge of good and evil. Humans are always doing the thing we shouldn't do. We, through Adam, surrendered our will to a cursed being (Satan) and the world through him has continued to be under the curse. Genesis 3:6-7: *So when the woman saw that the tree was good for food, that it was pleasant to the eyes, and a tree desirable to make one wise, she took of its fruit and ate. She also gave to her husband with her, and he ate. Then the eyes of both of them were opened, and they knew that they were naked; and they sewed fig leaves together and made themselves coverings.*

Before God returns to the scene to state the curse that they were under, Adam and Eve already felt the shame and sting of the betrayal. The curse had already fallen. Then, when God returned to the garden after Eve and Adam had eaten the apple, He simply stated the curse they were now under:

> *Then to Adam He said,*
> *"Because you have heeded the voice of your wife,*
> *and have eaten from the tree*
> *of which I commanded you, saying,*
> *'You shall not eat of it':*
> *"Cursed is the ground for your sake;*
> *In toil you shall eat of it*
> *All the days of your life.*
> *Both thorns and thistles*
> *it shall bring forth for you,*
> *And you shall eat the herb of the field.*
> *In the sweat of your face you shall eat bread*
> *Till you return to the ground,*
> *For out of it you were taken;*

For dust you are,
And to dust you shall return."

Genesis 3:17-19

It was because of what they had done that the ground was cursed.

In 2003 we walked across ground that was cursed for Adam's sake. Some of the pain and hardship of that crossing came from our own doing (I chose to start a light park) but the loss of Zoe was part of the curse that is on this world until Jesus returns. Then death itself will finally be put underfoot.

As painful as it was, though, we weren't alone. God kept great people near us to take us through this desert place. Andy and Julie Taylor were spiritual parents who patiently and gently walked with us. Lynn and Dorette Schaal gave us encouragement and comfort. Even when we were alone, the Father brought peace and joy out of the heartbreak and despair.

Jesus was, after all, very familiar with heartbreak. He cried over the people of Jerusalem who would not follow. He experienced the cross for us. He felt the agony of the blackness of grief that covers our eyes until we cry out "my God, my God why have you forsaken me." (from the Message) Hebrews 4:14-16: *He's been through weakness and testing, experienced it all—all but the sin. So let's walk right up to him and get what he is so ready to give. Take the mercy, accept the help.*

We had experienced the tribulation that Jesus had said we would experience. We came through it, and we began to realize we could be of good cheer because Jesus had overcome the world. The Light did really shine out of the darkness and the darkness really couldn't overcome it. Furthermore, faith could come and be the substance of what was hoped for. Tierney's birth was in many ways even more profound and impactful than the boys'. Yes, when they were born, our hearts leapt and grew within our chests and those moments were powerful. Yet somehow the darkness coming so near in the loss of Zoe made the light of Tierney's birth even brighter due to its contrast to the shadow of death.

God had taken us to another good pasture where we were becoming more substantial sheep. Sheep who were now ready to meet a new challenge at Sky Ranch, and sheep who knew the grace of God in a deeper and more profound way.

WHAT I LEARNED LATER

"God is good all the time and all the time God is good." This is something that is often quoted and repeated in churches around the country. I have said it many times myself, but without hard times this can only be a theory. Until we walk with God through something truly difficult, we can never really experience the truth of this statement. The Lord's light and grace are not diminished by challenges, they are highlighted by them. We fear the dark entirely too much. We hide our sin and our frailties; we push them down and lock them in a room, afraid the world will see our brokenness. Religion tells us to look good, to be a "good Christian", to never show any weakness. But God says that His strength is actually made perfect in our weakness. As hard as this period was, now I treasure it. It is when I saw God in some magnificent ways. It is when my own faith became deeper and more substantial, and it is where I saw even more clearly the goodness of Almighty God.

CHAPTER 13

$2$005 was a bit of a roundabout trip to Sky Ranch. It was difficult to get our minds around the idea of not competing for a living anymore. I spent the first half of the year trying to get a team in place at Sky Ranch and trying to compete at the rodeos. Consequently, my mind and effort were divided, and I didn't do either very well. Finally, in August I came home from the road and put all my effort into creating a successful and comprehensive equine program at Sky Ranch. They had asked me if I could take the horse program from being just an activity to be a point of ministry. We began by having our first event that fall. We had a beginner roping clinic. We took 20 kids who had never swung a rope and over a weekend helped these 7-11 year-old kids learn to rope a calf sled from the back of a horse. By doing the clinic with excellence, we were given the credibility and the opportunity to tell them about the love and salvation in Jesus Christ.

The clinic was great, but we needed an arena if we were going to seriously change the culture and begin to do rodeo clinics on a larger scale at Sky Ranch. Fortunately, God brought a couple of people who saw the vision and the value and who had the ability to help. Doug Collins donated all the pipe and RPR construction donated the dirt work. We had a 130'x330' arena with great sand and we began to plan our first Champions Rodeo Camp for the summer of 2006.

During the summer of 2006, Candice and I were able to implement two changes to the horse program. We put on the first week long Champions Rodeo Camp—no small feat, but critical to laying the foundation for this new area of the Sky Ranch ministry. Second, we adapted the summer camp ministry curriculum to utilize during the regular trail rides – this allowed us to use the horse as a picture or a parable that related to the Bible study. The first year we took the small kids who were only being led on horseback and hung puzzle pieces in the tree. When each kid brought their piece back the pieces could all be put together to create a picture which illustrated the verse. More subtly - we all bring our small piece for God to make us into a display nation of His grace. It was simple and maybe even a little cheesy, but it was a start, and it was successful. Not every kid makes a connection with their counselor, but our wranglers began to connect with some of these kids on the fringe even leading some of them to know the Father. The horse program began to see ourselves as a frontier of Sky Ranch. We were reaching the kids who were the most distant, and we were able to fill beds on the ends of camp, beds which were previously not being filled and which, when empty, meant no ministry was taking place.

> FOR WHOM HE FOREKNEW, HE ALSO PREDESTINED TO BE CONFORMED TO THE IMAGE OF HIS SON, THAT HE MIGHT BE THE FIRSTBORN AMONG MANY BRETHREN. MOREOVER WHOM HE PREDESTINED, THESE HE ALSO CALLED; WHOM HE CALLED, THESE HE ALSO JUSTIFIED; AND WHOM HE JUSTIFIED, THESE HE ALSO GLORIFIED. (ROMANS 8:29-30)

Our first Champions camp was a great success. We had Charlie Kingsbury, Cody Custer, Janet Stover, Al Bach and Chad Masters as instructors. The band Branded came and did the music for us, and God did some amazing things in not only the kids' lives but in ours as well. It was so successful that we decided to add a camp for beginners at the end of that first summer. We named it Young Riders Camp.

The next spring, I moved my annual steer wrestling clinics to Sky Ranch. We had our second Champions camp and our second and third Young Riders. I also had a vision to produce a clinic for really talented, fully committed teenage rodeo athletes that would help prepare them for college rodeo and for the professional ranks. Student-athletes in other sports have coaches and camps they can attend which teach them better skill-sets, but which also teach them how to prepare, what to eat, how to exercise, and how to get noticed and signed by college coaches. I decided to have it during the Christmas break and call it Elite Rodeo Clinic. The first year we only had 7 students, but it was clear rodeo kids didn't have access to the type of training we offered, and they loved it.

As 2008 began, we were ready to try to raise money for an

indoor arena. Candice had an amazing idea. She said why don't we have an event and call it "Cowboys and Cowboys." Her idea was to have a dinner and auction and invite our World Champion rodeo friends along with some Dallas Cowboys that we knew. We had met some great Dallas Cowboys over the years and were fortunate enough to know some who loved Jesus and who were willing to help us try to raise money. Walt Garrison was the first to jump in. He was not only a great running back for the Dallas Cowboys, but he also competed in the steer wrestling in the PRCA. Chad Hennings, Bob Lilly, Tony Lucio, and many others made our first event an amazing success. We raised over $100,000 and we were well on our way to having an indoor arena to serve the kids coming to Sky for rodeo camps.

It took us another 18 months and some generous donors to get the rest of the money to build an indoor arena, but in December of 2010, we had our 3rd Annual Elite Rodeo Clinic in the newly built 48,000 square foot Champions Rodeo Arena. My life was dynamically different, but God had just as much grace in this new place as he had when I was still rodeoing for a living.

GOOD PASTURE

Now Elijah, who was from Tishbe in Gilead, told King Ahab, "As surely as the LORD, the God of Israel, lives—the God I serve—there will be no dew or rain during the next few years until I give the word!" Then the LORD said to Elijah, "Go to the east and hide by Kerith Brook, near where it enters the Jordan River. Drink from the brook and eat what the ravens bring you, for I have commanded them to bring you food." So Elijah did as the LORD told him and camped beside Kerith Brook, east of the Jordan. The ravens brought him bread and meat each morning and evening, and he drank from the brook. But after a while the brook dried up, for there was no rainfall anywhere in the land.

1 Kings 17:1-7

Part of following God is realizing that He might bring you to a place where He supplies your needs, sometimes even miraculously. Then the supply may dry up. The question becomes whether you are trusting the supply or trusting God? Imagine Elijah. He was watching daily as the Lord met his needs in an amazing way, but then it began to dry up. I am sure he probably asked himself, "what did I do wrong, the brook is drying up?" I had this feeling more than once during this period. I felt like this in 2005. The brook that God had supplied my family with so regularly and dramatically through the years was beginning to dry up. I got esophagitis which constricted the bottom of my esophagus and caused me to lose over 30 pounds. Consequently, the rodeoing wasn't going well. But more than the lack of winning or the illness, the dryness was more a dryness of the spirit. I just wasn't loving what I was doing. I am sure Elijah followed quicker than I did, but you must wonder if he scratched his head a little bit when he heard what God wanted him to do next.

> *Then the LORD said to Elijah, "Go and live*
> *in the village of Zarephath, near the city of Sidon.*
> *I have instructed a widow there to feed you." So he went to*
> *Zarephath. As he arrived at the gates of the village, he saw a*
> *widow gathering sticks, and he asked her, "Would you please bring*
> *me a little water in a cup?" As she was going to get it, he called to*
> *her, "Bring me a bite of bread, too." But she said, "I swear by the*
> *LORD your God that I don't have a single piece of bread in the*
> *house. And I have only a handful of flour left in the jar and a little*
> *cooking oil in the bottom of the jug. I was just gathering a few*
> *sticks to cook this last meal, and then my son and I will die." But*
> *Elijah said to her, "Don't be afraid! Go ahead and do just what*
> *you've said, but make a little bread for me first. Then use what's*
> *left to prepare a meal for yourself and your son. For this is what the*
> *LORD, the God of Israel, says: There will always be flour and olive*
> *oil left in your containers until the time when the LORD sends*
> *rain and the crops grow again!" So she did as Elijah said, and she*
> *and Elijah and her family continued to eat for many days. There*

was always enough flour and olive oil left in the containers,
just as the LORD had promised through Elijah.

1 Kings 17:8-16

"Really God you want me to walk 80 miles and find a widow to meet my needs?" It is hard to walk away from the places where God has blessed you in the past. Even harder when those things have been a big part of your life for a long time. Even though rodeo is not what most people would call a comfortable life, to me it was as comfortable as an old pair of shoes. Then for God to bring something completely out of left field and for it to start in a kind of broken, unusual way made it hard to follow. However, when I did start to follow, God showed up in a miraculous way again.

WHAT I LEARNED LATER

Then God said, "Let Us make man in Our image, according
to Our likeness; let them have dominion over the fish of the
sea, over the birds of the air, and over the cattle, over all the
earth and over every creeping thing that creeps on the earth."
So God created man in His own image; in the image of God
He created him; male and female He created them. Then
God blessed them, and God said to them, "Be fruitful and
multiply; fill the earth and subdue it; have dominion over
the fish of the sea, over the birds of the air, and over every
living thing that [h]moves on the earth." And God said, "See,
I have given you every herb that yields seed which is on the
face of all the earth, and every tree whose fruit yields seed;
to you it shall be for food. Also, to every beast of the earth,
to every bird of the air, and to everything that creeps on the
earth, in which there is life, I have given every green herb for
food"; and it was so. Then God saw everything that He had
made, and indeed it was very good. So, the evening and the
morning were the sixth day.

Genesis 1:26-28

This passage is from before the fall of man. Notice how much there is to do. Man is to be fruitful and multiply. Tell me raising kids isn't work. Man is to fill the earth. It is a big earth. Man is to subdue the earth. There is a lot of wild country out there. Man is to have dominion or reign over all the fish, the birds, and the animals. That means we are building boats, husbanding all the animals, ranching…that is a lot of work. Man is to farm all the trees and the crops, and he is to use them to feed himself and the animals. That means he is a farmer which again entails a lot of work. In other words, WORK is from before Adam and Eve sinned. God requests all this work and says it is not only good but very good. I realize that after the fall, the work got a lot harder, but it doesn't take away the fact that work is a very good gift from the Father. Work is a gift! It is one of the ways we get to taste a bit of what it is like to be made in the image of our Heavenly Father, as Jesus says in John 5:17 But Jesus answered them, "My Father has been working until now, and I have been working." When we put our hands to the things God puts in front of us when we finish the day we get a glimpse of the Creator in us. When we built the two arenas, it was a lot of work. We would dig post-holes, set posts, weld top rails, then side rails. At the end of the day though we could look back and see what had been created. Work is a blessing and a gift whether it is manual labor or a column of numbers on a spreadsheet. We get to bring order out of chaos, we create something where there was nothing just like our Daddy. Gen 1:1, *When God began creating the heavens and the earth, the earth was a shapeless, chaotic mass ….**

We may at times complain about our jobs or the work we must do but we also know that nothing can make us as tired at times as doing nothing. After a hard day's work, we can end the day worn out but still feeling alive and empowered. Work is vital to the health and vitality of our mind, body, soul and spirit.

Chapter 14

In November of 2010, I was to turn 40. Candice and I had never really "tried" to have kids she just occasionally became pregnant. We both felt like we weren't sure if we were done but we had decided since Candice and I have the same birthday (November 17) that on the birthday when I turned 40 we were going to officially stop trying to have children. We had made this agreement about 18 months earlier after Candice had experienced another miscarriage. This one was earlier and a little less traumatic nevertheless it was a bumpy couple of months. Afterward, we decided we would continue to wait until November 17, 2010. We hadn't thought about this in some time, so when the day arrived, I was in Van at home with the kids and Candice was in Sayre, OK helping Andy Taylor with a ministry conference at Trinity. She was doing the music the night of our birthday, so I waited to call after the service. When I had her on the phone, I could hear in her voice that she had experienced something that night which had her excited and anxious. Candice began to tell me about a moment that took place after the service. She was sitting in the back of the church in just a quiet moment of worship and connection with the Father, and one of the speakers at the conference, a guy named David Van Cronkite came over to her with another lady from the church and asked her if he could tell her something he believed the Father told him to tell her. Candice said he could, and David began. He said "as I watched you sitting there worshipping the Lord in my mind's eye I saw your hair growing longer and your belly swelling as if you were pregnant" at this point Candice kind of gave a nervous laugh. David said "I don't know maybe you are beyond that in the natural. I just want to tell you what I believe the Father said after that." Then David said this, and this is what Candice wrote down, "God wants you to know this 'though you have had two miscarriages what is being born in you now is of Me and I will watch over it to completion.'" When Candice told me this we were both excited because at the time Candice had begun to have an idea about a children's TV show. We both thought it was a confirmation that the show was an idea from Heaven and God was going to bring it to pass. Neither of us considered the possibility that this was about an actual baby.

> BEHOLD, CHILDREN ARE A HERITAGE FROM THE LORD, THE FRUIT OF THE WOMB IS A REWARD. LIKE ARROWS IN THE HAND OF A WARRIOR, SO ARE THE CHILDREN OF ONE'S YOUTH. HAPPY IS THE MAN WHO HAS HIS QUIVER FULL OF THEM; THEY SHALL NOT BE ASHAMED, BUT SHALL SPEAK WITH THEIR ENEMIES IN THE GATE. (PSALMS 127:3-5)

Fast forward two weeks. I returned home in the evening from practicing with our boys and my wife was a little distraught and wanting to talk. She had her Bible open to where she wrote down what David had told her. Candice then reminded me of our plan to stop trying to get pregnant on my 40th birthday and that David had given her this message on our birthday. Then she showed me the pregnancy test. Candice began to cry. She went back over the whole story again, and as she came to the end of it, speaking of the baby, she said through tears "well I guess she will have a cool story to tell." As soon as Candice said this my heart leapt inside of my chest and I said "Oh! If it's a girl can we name her Storey?" Still crying and with me holding her in my arms she agreed that if it was a girl her name could be Storey.

God had brought us another child right under the wire. When David had spoken those words to her, Candice would have been less than 10 days pregnant no Doctor or pregnancy test would have been able to tell Candice was pregnant at that time, but God had known, and He had given us the Word on that day as if to say, "your plans crack me up." As the pregnancy progressed, we realized how much we needed this word from our Father. He had said this was from Him, and He would watch over it to completion, and we would really need the encouragement of those words. Candice was sick more with this child than with any of the previous children. She got a weird rash that the doctors couldn't identify. She began to spot early on which was what had happened with her two previous miscarriages. Her blood pressure began to elevate. Each of these things brought with them fear but each time our faith in what God had said rose up to meet that fear, and we were able to stand on the promise that what He had begun He would watch over to completion. I have always been head over heels in love with Candice, but I fell even more in love with her during this time. She was facing some things which would have robbed mighty men of their courage, but she faced them with grace and continued to be a positive hopeful mom to our other children, and she continued to be an amazing wife to me.

The day finally arrived in early August when she began labor and our beautiful daughter Storey was born on August 2nd, 2010.

Our family was almost complete.

I met Kevin Hayes when I was still a kid living in Kansas. He came to my dad's steer wrestling clinic and while he was a few years older than me we became friends at those clinics. He missed a steer badly at his second clinic and had to go to the hospital. Far from making him want to stop steer wrestling, he was more in than before. We have a five-clinics-and-you-are-free-for-life plan at our clinics and Kevin and his brother kept coming. They were from Indiana and after they came to one of our clinics in Texas, Kevin decided he wanted to move here with his family. He had two awesome boys and we got to watch Clay and Colt grow up here. When Colt was a little boy, there were two incidents which stood out in my mind to what an amazing and funny character he was. The first happened at my dad's house in Athens, TX. Kevin was down at a steer wrestling clinic and Colt was about 2 years old. He was playing in the grass and a fire ant bit him. Most kids would have run screaming, but not Colt. He stood in the middle of the fire ant mound and was stomping and whacking the fire ants as they continued to bite him. I grabbed him up out of the pile, and Kevin and I knocked the fire ants off his pants and legs. Colt was crying, but he looked more mad than hurt. The second incident was when we went to a friend's house to break in a set of steers when Colt was five years old. Kevin and Colt had ridden in my dad's pickup, and my brother and I had ridden in mine. When Colt got out of their truck, he saw us and started running towards us. The two trucks were parked about 50 yards apart. As Colt ran towards us, a mean-looking cur dog ran out from under a trailer and came barking and growling at Colt. We were all too far away to stop the dog and we were sure he was about to get bit. When the dog came barking at Colt, he turned and ran right at him and began yelling at the dog. The dog's head went up, he looked confused, then he turned tail and ran. This little boy had stood his ground.

A few years later Kevin was diagnosed with melanoma and they told him he would only have 6-12 months to live. Kevin prayed and asked the Father if he could stay alive long enough to see his oldest son, Clay, graduate. Amazingly, Kevin stayed remarkably healthy for most of the next five years. So much so that most people didn't even realize he was sick until right at the very end. Kevin made it until the spring of Clay's senior year. I had promised Kevin I would keep an eye out on Colt and Clay, and I would make sure they had what they needed. In the fall of 2011, Colt asked if we would consider allowing him to live with us. He started the second semester of his sophomore year in our home and he became a key member of our family.

Good Pasture

> *Now the LORD spoke to Moses, saying: "Speak to the children of Israel, that they turn and camp before Pi Hahiroth, between Migdol and the sea, opposite Baal Zephon; you shall camp before it by the sea. For Pharaoh will say of the children of Israel, 'They are bewildered by the land; the wilderness has closed them in.' Then I will harden Pharaoh's heart, so that he will pursue them; and I will gain honor over Pharaoh and over all his army, that the Egyptians may know that I am the LORD." And they did so.*
> Exodus 14:1-4

Following the Father sometimes means walking along paths which, while they are under your feet, appear to be going the wrong way. The Lord asked the children of Israel to turn and camp in Migdol next to the Red Sea. In effect, this hemmed them in between the sea and the entire Egyptian army that was in pursuit. The Israelites responded as we typically do when being brought face to face with the fears which have held us captive in the past.

> *And when Pharaoh drew near, the children of Israel lifted their eyes, and behold, the Egyptians marched after them. So they were very afraid, and the children of Israel cried out to the LORD. Then they said to Moses, "Because there were no graves in Egypt, have you taken us away to die in the wilderness? Why have you so dealt with us, to bring us up out of Egypt? Is this not the word that we told you in Egypt, saying, 'Let us alone that we may serve the Egyptians'? For it would have been better for us to serve the Egyptians than that we should die in the wilderness."*
>
> Exodus 14:10-12

God brought us back to the place where we had felt tremendous defeat in the past. Then the Father brought those chariots of fear right up to our door. God intentionally brought them to a place that emboldened their enemies. But when the Father had them there, He spoke to them and made a way through.

> *And the LORD said to Moses, "Why do you cry to Me? Tell the children of Israel to go forward. But lift up your rod and stretch out your hand over the sea and divide it. And the children of Israel shall go on dry ground through the midst of the sea. And I indeed will harden the hearts of the Egyptians, and they shall follow them. So, I will gain honor over Pharaoh and over all his army, his chariots, and his horsemen. Then the Egyptians shall know that I am the LORD, when I have gained honor for Myself over Pharaoh, his chariots, and his horsemen."*
>
> Exodus 14:15-18

God doesn't just want to remove you from Egypt, He wants to remove any power Egypt has over us. God knows that even if He saves us from a fear, the fear can remain, and as long as the fear is present we are held in bondage to that fear. So, the Father brought us to all the fear that we had experienced with the two previous lost pregnancies and by speaking to us and then delivering us through our own Red Sea of sorts, He drowned the fear with its chariots and horsemen in the Red Sea of His Blood. Following the Father often includes these turns which seem at best haphazard and at worst perilously close to the things we fear most. But so many times, they are intended to set us free from those fears and to encourage us to trust in what He says.

What I Learned Later

Faith comes from hearing,
and hearing by the word of Christ.

Romans 10:17

A lot is said about healing with God and the Bible. A lot is said about faith. I don't want to open a full discussion about faith here, only this small piece. Faith comes by hearing. We really can only believe what God has spoken in our hearts. Some believe God doesn't heal. All I can say is Kevin believed God said He would keep him healthy until Clay graduated, and He did. Some think Kevin should have been able to believe better things and that if he could believe God for five years why not more. All I have to say is if faith comes by hearing, Kevin heard five years and that is exactly what he got. Then Kevin went home to be in Heaven with the Father.

We heard the Father through David and those words came to pass. We prayed when Candice was pregnant with Zoe, and we heard "the light shown out of the darkness and the darkness did not overcome it." It didn't happen the way we thought, but nonetheless, it happened just like He said.

Now when I am faced with something challenging or anything I need to or want to pray about, I try to remember that prayer is communication with the Father and the most important part of communication is listening, not speaking. This is especially true when that communication is with the God of the universe. If we will listen, He will speak to His sheep. When we hear, faith comes. That faith will then be grounded on the bedrock of what the Father said.

Chapter 15

In 2011 my son Layton qualified for the National Junior High School Rodeo Finals in the calf roping and the goat tying. Candice, Storey, Layton and I headed out for Gallup, New Mexico. It is a long drive from east Texas to Gallup, especially with kids and horses. As we were driving across New Mexico, Candice received an email looking for adventurous men in the western world who would like to compete in a new show on the History Channel. The show was to be called Full Metal Jousting and the concept involved taking 16 men and teaching them the sport of full-contact jousting. The reality series would host weekly competitions, tournament style, with the overall winner taking home $100,000. Candice read the email aloud and then said: "I am going to enter you." We both laughed but she continued to fill out the application. It was a pretty good joke until 2 days later when a producer from the show called me to ask me some more questions. They then sent me a longer questionnaire which we filled out, still not really taking the whole thing seriously.

A week later the producer called back and asked if I could send them a video of me speaking into the camera and riding my horse. I sent a short video and the following week they asked me to fly to Los Angeles for another interview and a battery of tests including a full body MRI. At this point, I decided I better start taking this seriously. I went on the internet to try and find out what full-contact jousting was. This isn't renaissance faire and dinner theater jousting. For those venues, they use balsa wood lances, theater armor with 21st-century padding and the matches are basically choreographed. Full contact jousting uses inch and a half solid wood lances colliding into authentic armor, with real hits and real injuries.

When I went to LA for the audition, we were each instructed to have no contact with the other jousters, so I spent most of the 4 days walking the streets around the hotel and praying. I kept asking

God if this was something He wanted me to do. The answer kept coming back, yes. Two weeks later they called and asked if they could fly me to Jackson, Mississippi for a training week to see if I could make the show. The training was grueling. We spent most of the day riding draft horses and most of that time riding them bareback. I love riding horses but five hours a day riding extremely wide 2000-pound Percherons and Clydesdales was uncomfortable, to say the least. I felt like the training went well, but the instructors were not allowed to give any feedback, so it was impossible to tell whether I had done enough to be invited back for the show. There were still three weeks' worth of training groups to come.

I flew home and went back to work with zero contact from the producers. I had about come to the conclusion that I didn't make the cut when they called and said the show would start in a week and told me what to pack. I hurriedly prepared my Sky Ranch team for my absence and had some long talks with my wife and kids and got ready to be gone for a month. It all was happening so fast there was a real temptation to opt out of the whole thing, but God just kept giving us peace that I was supposed to do this.

I flew back to Jackson and all the men who were going to be on the show were in the same hotel for a final meeting with the production crew. The following morning, they put us in vans and drove us to the farm near Clinton, Mississippi. When we stepped out of the van, the cameras were rolling.

After the coaches picked teams, the first thing they did was put us in our armor and had us ride down the lyst as fast as we could. Halfway down the lyst a coach was standing on a platform with an aluminum baseball bat filled with lead shot. As we rode by the coach would swing the bat and hit us in the chest. Then after doing this several times, they explained to us that this was a small collision compared to the real shots from a lance.

After practice, we returned to the two apartments (black team and red team). This is where I began to see why the Father may have wanted me to be on this show. We were not allowed to bring anything to read with us except "religious materials." I was the only guy to bring a Bible and one guy on the red team brought a book on Buddhism. I was with a group of 16 men—only two of us were professing believers—and we were going to live with each other day in and day out for over a month.

Our days were set with three hours of training in the morning and three hours in the afternoon. The rest of the time we were left to eat, drink and hang out together in the two apartments and the area around the barns. We played thousands of games of Spades. I cooked most of the meals for my team. I usually woke them up in the morning made breakfast and prepared for the day. The show took on a three-day week schedule. They would get us up early on day one and take us to a field and a stage where the coaches would pick their matchup. Then we would begin two days of preparing our member from the black team for his joust. There were three of us on the black team that became known as the Three Stooges. Jack Mathers, Josh Knowles, and I were called that because we broke more stuff than the Stooges. We would jump in the lyst and start trading blows with our teammates at the drop of a hat. Typically, the coaches would put one of us into the lyst to help prepare the black team competitor who was up next against the red team. Some of those practices were pretty epic. The biggest failure of the show, in my opinion, was they should have shown more of our black team practices. We would usually break all the lances they had prepared for us. We had one practice where Tom aimed low with his lance and he hit Matt Hiltman in the nether regions. Matt had to be hauled to the hospital to get stitches. Then Josh Knowles entered the lyst. On the second pass, Tom shot low again and Josh was headed to the hospital for stitches. The show must go on, so they asked me to get in the lyst with Tom. I joked "is this because I already have five kids?" The first pass down I smoked Tom and nearly unhorsed him. Then our coaches asked me if I would ride down the lyst without a lance and just let Tom take some target practice on me. Of course, I did.

The show was like getting 15 brothers and then being forced into close proximity with no distractions. It showed me how important people are. I learned that while some in the group had personalities that were difficult for me, once I took the time to really know them I usually found some common ground. While I couldn't always agree with their thoughts and behaviors, I came to respect them as brothers and could see even their annoying behaviors as by-products of the story God was telling through them. I realized how each of them was an opportunity to show some patience and kindness.

As far as the jousting went, I won my first match then lost to Josh Avery by 1 point in my second match. In a surprise move by the producers, I was invited back and won the $25,000 consolation match. We all felt like we never really got to do our very best in the matches, mostly because the match lyst was set up for TV with cameras whirring overhead which really spooked the horses. The matches had these weird delays which had a tendency to throw off our timing. It just wasn't as good as the jousting we did during the practice sessions. However, eight of the guys from the show did get another opportunity to show what we could do. As the show was airing that winter, they brought 8 of us to Madison, Wisconsin to the Midwest Horse Fair to compete in the Armored All-Star Challenge. We had an eight-man tournament each day with the winner taking home $10,000. It was epic! We broke lances right and left. Josh Knowles, the Full Metal Jousting champion and I went head to head in an awesome match. I ended up unhorsing him for a 35-21 point victory.

I got to know some incredible men during the 38 days we were together on the show. I was able to pray on national TV for my kids and my family. I learned a lot about myself, and I got a much deeper view of the Father's heart. I am very thankful for the opportunity the Father gave me, the people I met, and the adventure I got to take.

Good Pasture

This experience left me with a saying. "You never know where your feet will take you if you give them to God." This was a very different pasture than I ever thought I would find but God knew me, and He knew there was some very specific grass with some very exact nutrients that I needed if I was going to be the sheep He is leading me to be. In a relatively short period of time the Father radically changed my perspective about people. Because I knew the world to be the pen of the sheep and a place where sheep can never realize who they were meant to be, I had begun to see the sheep trapped in their own pen as flawed and broken. People are flawed and broken, but they are so much more. Even at their worst, they have incredible abilities, beautiful dreams, and immense potential. People are not their sin. We unconsciously are siding with the devil when we identify the thief as a thief. We must look deeper the way the Father does. I do not show people to the gate when I remind them they are sinners. I only help keep their eyes on the brokenness which already defines their lives. With the Father's help, I can see past the smudge to the masterpiece beneath. Jesus sees the persecution of Paul but sees past it to the man within and He sees what is possible when that life is surrendered to Him. 1 John 3:1-3: *Behold what manner of love the Father has bestowed on us, that we should be called children of [a]God! Therefore the world does not know [b]us, because it did not know Him. Beloved, now we are children of God; and it has not yet been revealed what we shall be, but we know that when He is revealed, we shall be like Him, for we shall see Him as He is. And everyone who has this hope in Him purifies himself, just as He is pure.*

While we are trying to "fix" people, God is wanting us to let them know their Father loves them. Jesus knows that when He is revealed they shall want to be like He is because they will see Him as He is. Everyone who receives this hope will purify themselves. We won't need to do any fixing.

I am so thankful the Good Shepherd led me to this mountain valley. I see people differently now.

What I Learned Later

Blessed be the God and Father of our Lord Jesus Christ, who has blessed us with every spiritual blessing in the heavenly places in Christ, just as He chose us in Him before the foundation of the world, that we should be holy and without blame before Him in love, having predestined us to adoption as sons by Jesus Christ to Himself, according to the good pleasure of His will, to the praise of the glory of His grace, by which He made us accepted in the Beloved.
Ephesians 1:3-6

Jesus paid the price for everyone to receive the adoption as sons. So, if my Father purchased the lost as His sons and daughters, then they must all be my brothers and sisters. After Colt moved into our home, we began to treat him as our son. As far as we are concerned he is our boy. However, Colt had to choose to accept us as his people who could parent him. If Colt had never chosen to accept us, it wouldn't have changed how we felt about him.

Many believers have divided people into two or three groups. It is either believers and non-believers, or it is sinners, saints and enemies of the Cross. I don't believe it is this way with the Father. Jesus paid the price for all to become God's children. John 3:16 *"For God so loved the world that He gave His only begotten Son, that whoever believes in Him should not perish but have everlasting life."* Whoever believes. John 1:12-13 says: *"But as many as received Him, to them He gave the right to become children of God, to those who believe in His name: who were born, not of blood, nor of the will of the flesh, nor of the will of man, but of God. As many as received Him who believed He gave the right to be children of God."*

As a simple human, I cannot tell where people are when it comes to whether they have accepted God's offer of sonship. What I do know is my Father wants them to be His kids. God wants to adopt them, so I have the ability to start treating them as my brothers and sisters. I don't need to separate them into groups. This separating has always been a ploy of the enemy. He always

116

wants to separate and dehumanize. If I call people nonbelievers or "the lost" or sinners, then I have made two separate groups and separate is never equal. I can do all sorts of bad things in the name of God if I dehumanize people by calling them "sinners" or "enemies of the Cross." No! Everyone is my brother and my sister, and I can treat them like they are even if they never choose to accept my Father.

For you did not receive the spirit of bondage again to fear,
but you received the Spirit of adoption by whom we cry out,
"Abba, Father." The Spirit Himself bears witness with our
spirit that we are children of God, and if children, then
heirs—heirs of God and joint heirs with Christ, if indeed we
suffer with Him, that we may also be glorified together.
Romans 8:15-17

CHAPTER 16

If God would have wanted something other than a family, He would have called Himself something other than Father.

God has blessed me with an amazing family. I have incredible cousins, aunts, uncles and grandparents. All of them have shown me pieces of the Father in their love, encouragement, kindness, and care. The Myers and DeArmond's are a passionate bunch of people who passionately pursue their dreams. They take family seriously in a very fun way. One of my earliest memories is going to a family reunion at my uncle Chet and aunt Mary's place in Castle Rock, Colorado. A deep sense of belonging came with hanging with the cousins, playing, enjoying each other and the opportunity to be together. Neither my dad nor my mom came from people who went to church, but both of their parents put a premium on family. Most of my kin have become believers and the roots of a people who loved each other, who stayed and worked through hard times has made their walk with Christ a simple transition. It hasn't always been easy, but they have kept it simple.

> AGAIN, THE KINGDOM OF HEAVEN IS LIKE TREASURE HIDDEN IN A FIELD, WHICH A MAN FOUND AND HID; AND FOR JOY OVER IT HE GOES AND SELLS ALL THAT HE HAS AND BUYS THAT FIELD.

I have an amazing sister! Tygh is maybe the most fiercely loyal person I know. We might fight and she might even get angry with me, but I always knew she had my back unequivocally. Tygh and I are only 14 months apart, and we grew up traveling a lot with our parents. We would travel all around the country to rodeos and we had some other kids who we would see at the rodeos, but Tygh was my closest friend. She is an incredible mom who protects her family like a lioness. If you make a friend of Tygh, you have made a friend for life and a friend who will not leave in times of adversity. Proverbs 17:17: *A friend loves at all times, and a brother (or sister) is born for adversity.*

I have an awesome brother! Cash is a doer. Cash amazes me; he has successfully launched multiple businesses. He bought and ran a feed store, he built and ran a construction company, he has a successful rodeo clinic business, he makes money as an insurance adjuster. All of these, Cash has done while winning championships in the arena, and raising four incredibly talented kids. My kids have always liked their uncle Cash. He can get the fun started in about 30 seconds. This hit-the-ground running attitude of his inspires me and many others to trust that anything is possible we merely need to put our hand to the plow.

From both sides of my family, I learned toughness and kindness. But none modeled those two Christlike attributes more genuinely and consistently than my mom. When I was small, my mom would teach kids all day then come home, saddle, and train barrel horses, open chutes for my dad, make sure my sister and I had everything we needed (horse saddled, snack, homework done...). Then she would have dinner ready before we all finished our day. She worked extremely hard, but she never seemed to be grouchy or not to have the time for anything we needed. I remember this pair of coveralls that my mom had which were like three sizes too big, she would be out feeding cattle in the freezing Kansas wintertime. Her face and nose would be bright red, but she would still be smiling. My dad was a world champion and known all over the United States, still when I was on the road nearly as many people would ask me about my mom. She had that effect because she was always kind. It didn't matter who you were, my mom had time for you, and she would give you her best. Mom was tough, and she could jerk down a switch and give you a whipping in a hurry if you needed it, but her toughness was always tempered by a truly kind heart.

Dad has always been my biggest hero. A guy named Greg came from Australia to live with my dad, work for him and learn to steer wrestle. One day we were building a barn on my dad's place, my dad was going extremely hard and fast trying to get the job done when Greg said to my father, "Butch you know Rome wasn't built in a day." When he finished saying this, my dad just looked at Greg. A moment passed and Greg said, "well I guess you weren't there to build it." This scene sums up one of the greatest attributes of my father, and one of the ways he modeled the Father to me. My dad was not just a hard worker, he was also someone who knows how to enjoy the work he is doing. I remember growing up, I always wanted to go with my dad when he was working. Whether it was building fences, cleaning stalls, working cattle, or some other endeavor, I always wanted to be with him. He always made these difficult tasks seem less strenuous because he just did them without complaint or negativity. I look back at some of the truly difficult jobs we did, and the overwhelming emotion isn't the pain of the struggle but the joy of the accomplishment. I hesitate to call this a work ethic for that makes it seem like enduring something hard, when in reality, work with my dad, while challenging, seemed more of an honor than a chore. I am not saying I always looked at it this way; of course, there were times especially through my teen years where I dreaded it. However, this same pleasure in the task at hand found me later and I saw it in the way Jesus approached the cross. *Looking unto Jesus, the author and finisher of our faith, who for the joy that was set before Him endured the cross, despising the shame, and has sat down at the right hand of the throne of God.*

A willingness to work hard wasn't the only thing I received from my dad. The most valuable lesson I got from him was that I am loved. There have been very few days in my father's house where he didn't tell me he loved me. In a time when men are typically stoic and unaffectionate, my dad was the opposite. He would hug us and tell us he loved us and that he was proud of us. He wasn't always proud of the things we would do, but he was always proud of us. This form of unconditional love was empowering in my walk with my Heavenly Father. Knowing unconditional love from my dad made it easier to accept it from God.

GOOD PASTURE

It is not that they do not know the truth about God; indeed he has made it quite plain to them. For since the beginning of

the world the invisible attributes of God, e.g., his eternal
power and divinity, have been plainly discernible through
things which he has made and which are commonly seen
and known, thus leaving these men without a rag of
excuse. They knew all the time that there is a God, yet
they refused to acknowledge him as such, or to thank him
for what he is or does. Thus they became fatuous in their
argumentations, and plunged their silly minds still further
into the dark.

Romans 1:19-23

God can certainly be seen in creation. The hills, sky and stars tell of Him. In man, the pinnacle of His creation, we can see God too. When we open our eyes to the Father and when we stop worshipping the creation and begin to worship the creator, we can see God's power and divinity on display in the lives of people all around us. Jesus wants to be known. He knows that everything that pertains to life and Godliness is found in the knowledge of Him. God knows that all of the good and precious promises are found in knowing Him. The Father has put His breath into people and even when some of those people aren't following the Lord He still has instilled in them a piece of the divine. Sure, the supernatural in people can be covered and marred a bit by the corruption in the world, but if we have eyes to see it is still there. The Kingdom has always been within us; it is only waiting to be revealed. When I began to follow the leading of the Lord in my life, I began to see life on display all around me.

WHAT I LEARNED LATER

But this Man, after He had offered one sacrifice
for sins forever, sat down at the right hand of God, from
that time waiting till His enemies are made
His footstool. For by one offering He has perfected forever

*those who are being sanctified. For by that one offering he
forever made perfect those who are being made holy.*
Hebrews 10:12-14

In 2002 one of the places Candice and I were asked to go speak at was the Montana Circuit finals rodeo. While Candice was singing, God gave me this message. As I hastily scrambled to get what God wanted me to say Candice, sang an extra song to give me some more time.

He has perfected forever those who are being sanctified

The Holy spirit gave me the picture of a pure-bred cow and a pure-bred bull. Nothing can affect the purity of their birth, but as long as the fences of the pasture are down, their offspring can be called into question.

*Every good gift and every perfect gift is from above, and
comes down from the Father of lights, with whom there is no
variation or shadow of turning.*
James 2:3

*God has dealt to each one a measure of faith.
For as we have many members in one body,
but all the members do not have the same function, so we,
being many, are one body in Christ,
and individually members of one another.
Having then gifts differing according to the grace that is given
to us, let us use them: if prophecy,
let us prophesy in proportion to our faith; or ministry, let us
use it in our ministering; he who teaches,
in teaching; he who exhorts, in exhortation; he who gives,
with liberality; he who leads, with diligence;
he who shows mercy, with cheerfulness.*
Romans 12:3-8

The good things in our lives come from the Father. He gives gifts to all men. Not just to the saved. We all know people who aren't Christians who are excellent leaders, givers, exhorters ... For the purposes of this let's call these gifts pure blood Angus heifers. We all have good gifts in our lives, but our fences are torn down, and the world is in our pasture (life). Coyotes are in our pasture stealing the offspring, the production from our gifts. We have all sorts of ill-bred bulls in our pasture breeding with these gifts producing offspring which never turn out as we want. These other bulls introduce diseases into our herd. They abuse our heifers until they become wild and out of control.

Hopefully, somewhere along the way, we are introduced to Jesus and when we receive Him we receive the Perfect herd Bull. The new life we receive is the incorruptible Seed. He perfects us on the inside, but our fences are still down. We are still in need of sanctification. (To be sanctified is to be set apart or to be fenced off.) The issue is how we go about the sanctification process. Religion makes us fence-menders. We run from hole to hole in the fence constantly looking out for the newest tear in our defenses. We become scared Christians always aware of all the problems and sin in our lives and paying very little attention to our herd bull. However, if we keep our eyes on Jesus the author and finisher of our faith, we begin to bring these good gifts(heifers) to our herd Bull. He gently and in the right times begins to impregnate the gifts in our lives with Himself. Then our life begins to produce Life. Sometimes it produces another heifer calf which God will give us an opportunity to share that gift with others. For instance, I might have the chance to show someone how to steer wrestle or how to weld or any number of things which to the recipient can become a good gift in their life. At other times this union between the gifts God has given us and the life He has given us in Jesus will produce a male offspring in the form of God allowing us to share Jesus with another person. When they receive Him, another person receives a herd bull to give life to their world.

*Let us hold tightly without wavering to the hope
we affirm, for God can be trusted to keep his promise. Let us
think of ways to motivate one another to acts of love and good*

works. And let us not neglect
our meeting together, as some people do,
but encourage one another, especially now
that the day of his return is drawing near.

Hebrews 10:23-25

So, we hold tightly without wavering to our herd bull and we gather together with other believers, and when we do this, we encourage each other, and we build each other's fences.

CHAPTER 17

I have the greatest kids anyone could ever ask for. Each one of them is unique, gifted, compassionate, and wonderful. Each one is an amazing example of the character and nature of Jesus.

LAYTON

The summer of 2018, Layton worked as a family camp counselor at Sky Ranch Ute Trail. I can't tell you how many times I have been somewhere over the last year and someone has asked me "Are you Layton's dad?" Inevitably it is because he was their family camp counselor last summer. They then go on describing in great detail how amazing Layton Myers is, which of course comes as no surprise to me. From the beginning, Layton was this amazing combination of kindness and strength. He has the ability to meet hard moments with a fierce determination while at the same time being kind to all of the people who are near him even in the heat of the moment. When Layton was about 10 or 11 years old, he was playing in a big select baseball tournament. His team was down 2 runs in the bottom of the last inning. There were two runners on base, and he had two strikes. He smokes a line drive towards right field, and it looks like it is going to get down when the other team's right fielder makes an amazing diving catch, and they lose the game. He was heartbroken. He felt like he had let his team down. Candice and I were consoling him over lunch when I saw the kingdom in him so clearly. He was upset not because he failed but because he had let his teammates down. Layton was able to dare to swing for the fences in that tense moment not for his own glory but for the benefit of his team. This courage and selflessness have always been a trademark of Layton's life.

Layton is known for his kindness, but to those of us who know him best we see the rod of titanium inside of that kind exterior which gives him the power like our Savior to endure the cross and despise its shame for the joy in people set before him.

HE GIVES POWER TO THE WEAK AND STRENGTH TO THE POWERLESS. EVEN YOUTHS WILL BECOME WEAK AND TIRED, AND YOUNG MEN WILL FALL IN EXHAUSTION. BUT THOSE WHO TRUST IN THE LORD WILL FIND NEW STRENGTH. THEY WILL SOAR HIGH ON WINGS LIKE EAGLES. THEY WILL RUN AND NOT GROW WEARY. THEY WILL WALK AND NOT FAINT.

Holden

Most people are driven and controlled the majority of their lives by fear. They are afraid of what others think. They are afraid to fail. They are afraid to risk. Holden may be the least affected by fear of anyone I know. Holden really isn't concerned with what others think of him, and though he doesn't like to fail he isn't afraid of it either. Holden tries to live his life by his internal compass. It means as his parents there have been times when he turned to the right or the left and it left his parents a little shaken. However, although we didn't know if he was making the right decision we always knew Holden was making the decision because he truly believed it was right, and it wasn't motivated by fear.

The clearest example of this was during his junior year of high school. The high school rodeo season was at the halfway point, and we were leaving the following morning to drive to Graham, Texas for Holden to compete. At 10:00 o'clock pm Holden walks into my bedroom and declares that he doesn't want to go and is quitting rodeo to commit completely to basketball in the effort to secure a scholarship. I was dumbstruck! Holden was sitting first in the steer wrestling and fourth in the calf roping with a good chance to make it to Nationals in both events. I wanted to be upset and to make him change his mind because I definitely thought it was a mistake. I was in the bedroom trying to decide what to say to get him to change his mind when I clearly heard the Father say to me in the still, small voice, "Do you trust that I am his God?" So, I swallowed hard and went to the rodeo the following day without him. Holden worked his tail off to get a scholarship to play basketball in college. He had several offers and once again took a left turn. When his senior season was complete, he surprised Candice and me again by declaring he wasn't going to take any of the scholarship offers because none of the schools that had offered him scholarships had an aviation program.

Holden declared for Southeastern Oklahoma State and began to fly planes. He then came home at the end of his freshmen year with great grades and said, "I think I am going to go out for the rodeo team." He still wanted to continue to get his aviation degree, but he wanted to rodeo as well. In each of these decisions, Holden chose to turn not from a sense of fear or out of any obligation to meet other's expectations; he turned because he felt sure each decision was what the Father wanted him to do. He may or may not have heard correctly each time. That isn't the point. The important thing was he believed, and he followed.

Holden continues to be an example to me of what it means to follow the voice of the Shepherd.

TIERNEY

I am in awe of my daughter Tierney. She is beautiful without being vain. She is intelligent yet remains a learner. She is gifted still she is humble. She is a giver without seeking praise. She is bold yet not pushy. And she is a follower of Jesus without being religious.

One of Tierney's greatest gifts is that she loves, so she gives. For God so loved the world that He gave. Tierney goes all-in on everything she does. She loves her brothers and they love basketball. So, she gives herself to know basketball for in doing so she will have the opportunity to enhance her relationship with her brothers. Tierney is now a huge Houston Rockets fan. Because if she is going to do anything, she is going to do it all the way. Tierney wants to go on the class trip to Washington DC. We ask her to raise half of the money, so she decides to start making cakes to pay for the trip. What started as a small fundraising effort, turned into a small home-based business that blessed so many people. She still gives a lot of cakes away even though they take her quite a bit of time to complete. From the time she was in Kindergarten I have said she should be on the payroll at the school because the teachers are daily asking her to do something for them. The teachers know Tierney will not just give them the help they need, but they know she will do it with excellence. Like our Savior Tierney gives of herself willingly, continually, excellently, and extravagantly.

STOREY

I am torn between which attribute of Storey's most clearly shows me a picture of Jesus. On one hand, Storey has a quiet confidence which gives her a peace or serenity which helps her thrive, and on the other hand, she also has extreme compassion which sometimes sweeps her up and brings her to tears for the plight of others.

A few years ago, I had the bright idea to take my family to see *A Dog's Purpose*. This is a pretty heart-wrenching movie to begin with. (Spoiler alert: The dog dies like a lot of times.) It was tough for all my kids but poor Storey was almost inconsolable. The same thing happened in the live version of Beauty and the Beast; she was crying nearly uncontrollably when she thought the beast had died. It's not just at movies either. Storey has a natural compassion for others which reminds me of the way Jesus looked at the people, and the Bible says He had compassion for them. Storey gives me a visible image of what that compassion looks like in a tiny human form.

Her confidence was front and center when she was on her baseball team last year. She was in her first season of machine pitch, and while she was doing well, the place where I saw this "peace born out of confidence" best displayed was in the dugout. She would encourage a teammate who had struck out, correct an older girl who wasn't being kind, cheer on another teammate who got a hit, then calmly walk to the batter's box and stroke the ball or lay down a bunt without even the slightest notion of nervousness or tension. It is the kind of peace that allowed Jesus to sleep in the bow of the boat in the middle of a storm. Storey has that type of peace and strength.

GOOD PASTURE

The Father continuously uses my children to lead me into a different and deeper relationship with Him. Wherever we are and no matter what we are doing, God will surprise me with a glimpse into my life through the looking glass of my kids. Sometimes it's a taste of how much He loves me by filling my heart to bursting with love for my children. Other times the Father will show me intimate things about myself in the faces of my kids. And still other times, He will bring scriptures into a whole new light while watching a parable played out in the lives of my sons and daughters.

With Layton at his birth, I saw maybe for the first time that love is unconditional. When he came into this world, I loved him before he had done anything. That changed my understanding of love. It certainly changed my idea of the Father's love for me. Also with Layton, God brought me to a deeper understanding of His love when Layton went through some trying times when he was in college. I realized that the love of the Father was ever predicated on our works. Until then I think there was a part of me which felt God's love for the lost was unconditional but that maybe He would have some conditions on His love once I became a believer.

Holden showed me the limitlessness of God's love. When Holden was born, I could feel my heart expand in my chest. The Father's love is not in part but complete, and all it needs to grow is more people to receive His affection. Jesus deepened my trust in Him with Holden. Holden had a relationship with the Father at an early age that was separate from me. That is a good thing but still, it requires trust of the Father and of my son because Holden wasn't coming to me for guidance like his brother had.

Tierney from birth began to break open entire floors of my personality which hadn't been entered in years before she became a part of our lives. With Tierney, the Father began to show me beauty and color. The first night as I listened to her sighs my ears were opened to hear a softer less urgent call from the Father. Life was more than just taking territory for the Kingdom, it was also about the beauty of the Kingdom and the power of the grace and beauty the Father had put there to draw others to that Kingdom.

With Storey, I am beginning to learn the high art of being present. This is a lesson the Father is currently teaching me, but Storey is a great teacher. I have realized recently that in my attempts to DO all the things that need to be done, I have not always been as present with my kids as I want to be. Storey makes me, and I am so thankful for that. She asks me to stop and listen to her story or to really look at her drawing. When she does, there is a part of me that hurts for my other kids because I can remember times when I continued to pick up or do the dishes when they were asking for my attention, and I only gave them some of it.

Chapter 18

Candice

From chapter 6 onwards Candice has been all over the story of my life. She is between the lines on the pages at the lead and behind the scenes of all the moments of my life since 1995. A chapter is not nearly enough to show all the ways the Father has used this incredible woman to help me know Him, to experience His love and to find the Good Pasture. Candice is a blessing to everyone who comes in contact with her, and I have been abundantly blessed with the opportunity to spend the last 24 years with her. Here is a very small sampling of the ways the Father has revealed His character and nature to me through her life.

> WHO CAN FIND A VIRTUOUS AND CAPABLE WIFE? SHE IS MORE PRECIOUS THAN RUBIES. HER HUSBAND CAN TRUST HER, AND SHE WILL GREATLY ENRICH HIS LIFE. SHE BRINGS HIM GOOD, NOT HARM, ALL THE DAYS OF HER LIFE.

When Candice and I were on our fourth date, we had an opportunity to have one of those long talks where we open up about our past and our history. I mentioned to her the way the few girls I had dated all seemed to hide a crazy past. Candice responded in a very unique way. She said, "well then you will not want to hang around with me." She then proceeded to tell me some very difficult things that had happened to her in her past and with her family. Quite the opposite of running me away this actually drew me to her. This honesty was so refreshing. I found myself telling her things from my past that I never would have dreamed of telling a girl especially on only the 4th date.

Good Pasture

And the Word became flesh and dwelt among us,
and we beheld His glory, the glory as of the only begotten of

the Father, full of grace and truth.
And of His fullness we have all received, and grace for grace.
For the law was given through Moses, but grace and truth
came through Jesus Christ. No one has seen God at any time.
The only begotten Son, who is in the bosom of the Father,
He has declared Him.

John 1:14-18

In order to follow the "Light of the world" you can't be someone who wants to keep things in the dark. Our past, our mess is plain for him to see, but shame keeps us in the place of always wanting to hide or cover that shame. We fail to realize that grace and truth are intimately connected. We can't receive grace until we abide in the truth and there is nothing as powerful as grace to draw the truth out of us. Truth is vitally important to Candice, and if God had never brought her into my life, I would have never fallen in love with the truth which means it would have been difficult to know The Way, The Truth, and the Light.

WHAT I LEARNED LATER

Brene Brown has a talk she gives about courage, and in this speech, she connects two seemingly opposite virtues those of vulnerability and courage. She basically explains that without vulnerability no act can be courageous. Vulnerability is the quality or state of being exposed to the possibility of being attacked or harmed, either physically or emotionally. All courageous acts come from someone being exposed or vulnerable and rising above in that moment. Candice's vulnerability in that moment was incredibly courageous. She had to expose her heart to the opportunity for rejection. My wife is one of the most courageous people I know. Candice will have moments before the trial or obstacle where she may feel frightened or nervous, but in the fray when the battle arrives, no one is braver than she.

CANDICE

As we continued to date I would come to Candice's house in Weatherford and often I would walk to the grocery store which was only a few blocks away to pick up something for dinner. The first time I went, I saw a small pie, and I decided to grab it too. Candice had told me a story where she mentioned that she liked pie, so I brought one to her house. When I came in the door, I saw the delight she took not in the pie but in the gesture. So, every time I went to the store after that I would look around trying to find something to give her that would elicit delight in her.

GOOD PASTURE

The Father delights in our delight and the precious innocence which is found in the moment of surprise and delight. It cleanses our hearts and restores our youth. He has given me so many moments of pure delight. A moment when a sight takes your breath away or a song carries you to another place. The Father puts these tiny packages of His love in all sorts of moments for us to open at random times and in random places which when we will allow ourselves to experience them they will awaken in us passion, hope, courage, peace and all sorts of powerful life-giving emotions. The Father leaves these packages not as a way to try to control our behaviors like a man trying to lay out bait in order to lure some animal into his trap. I believe the Father gifts us with these moments of delight simply because giving is in His nature. These packages of delight aren't given to get a result from us but when they are truly received it is hard not to want to be nearer to the Giver.

WHAT I LEARNED LATER
(OR WHAT I AM STILL TRYING TO LEARN)

Much to my chagrin my gifts over the years have drawn less delight than they used to. This left me in a place where I began to think the fault was with Candice, that she had lost something for me or that she was ungrateful. Lately, however, I have begun to see that the trouble lies in me. In trying to elicit delight in her, I had stopped doing it for the sole purpose of her delight. I had begun to look for and enjoy the delight for myself. Boiled down to its rawest form, this is the difference between Agape or God's kind of love and any other kind of love. Agape is usually defined as unconditional love and that is what it is. However, the conditions we place on our love are not always on the front end. For instance, many times we think of Agape as the willingness and ability to love even those who revile us. In other words, we place no conditions on who we love. But Agape does more than that, it also places no conditions on the love we give after it has been sent. We ask for nothing in return not even that the love we have given must be received. A good pastor that I know, Dudley Hall, uses the illustration of a cane. He proceeds to point out that most of the love we give has a hook in it. A portion of the love we send we want to come back to us. Agape must be freely given, for that is how it was received. CS Lewis in his book The Four Loves points out that while God is love, love is not God and if we make even Agape our god even love can consume us. This was hard for me to understand for many years. Until recently when I began to see it with Candice. I was choosing to love her unconditionally, but I was disappointed when it wasn't received the way I had hoped it would be received. We don't realize that if any vestige of self remains in our love for others, in the end, the one who is robbed is us.

CANDICE

After we were married for several years and Candice had been singing at quite a few church services, she was preparing to do her first album. Candice wanted to write but hadn't had much success. Then one night we were sleeping in the trailer at a rodeo when Candice abruptly got out of bed and went into the restroom. I initially thought she was sick. However, after she assured me she was OK, I went back to sleep. In a couple of hours, she woke me up as she was getting back into bed. I asked her what she had been doing, she replied, "writing a song." When she sang the song to me for the first time, it was clear that the Father had breathed the song into her. It was a song that had come from some of her broken past, but it was full of restoration and hope. The tears were flowing as she finished singing it to me. You could feel the presence of the Lord in the trailer, and the words seemed to reach right into you and break and heal your heart.

GOOD PASTURE

Seeing the Father pour this song into Candice in such a clear and powerful way radically impacted my own walk with God. Before this, I believed the Father wanted to and would lead His children, but I don't think I really believed he would do it in such a powerful and moving way. I knew and had experienced the Father leading people during times of studying His Word when the lights come on and all of sudden you see something differently which changes your path, and you begin to get a clearer picture of who you are meant to become. I had seen and experienced the Lord moving people during worship where the Spirit moved me or others to release old hurts or to reach for new hopes. I intellectually understood that the Father wanted to lead His children, and I had experienced some of that leading, but for the first time, I saw how involved and intimate the Father wanted to be with us. If God would come into our horse trailer and spend a couple of hours in the bathroom pouring this powerful song into my wife's heart, maybe He wanted to speak into my life in similar ways. Not that He was going to help me write a song, but that He wanted to give clear guidance and inspiration for the plans, hopes and dreams in my heart.

WHAT I LEARNED LATER

My sheep hear My voice and to the stranger they will not heed.

When I began to really listen for the Father, I was often frustrated because it seemed like I seldom heard the still small voice. I never heard it when I was actively and intently listening for Him. Then after a day in the practice pen, I was driving home, and this verse came unbidden into my mind. All of a sudden it dawned on me that I was listening for a "strange" voice when Jesus had called me His friend, so the voice of the Father was no longer the voice of a stranger but the voice of a friend. As I let this truth begin to change me, I came to a deeper revelation. When I had been listening intently for the Father to give me some answer to a prayer or a question I had placed before Him I had been listening for the voice of a master instead of the voice of a Father. I was listening to hear demands like do this, go here, don't do that .... My ears weren't tuned into the voice of a Father who was there listening, encouraging, and asking questions that would reveal my own heart to me and give me the Light I needed to see my way. The Father is leading His children, His sheep, His friends to Good pasture so let's listen for a Father, a Good Shepherd, and a Friend.

Candice

Candice was pregnant with our second son and I had driven home from Cheyenne for the birth. We had scheduled to be induced on Monday morning. At 5:30 in the morning, I am driving my wife to the hospital and Candice is crying. I ask her what was the matter? She burst out "I don't think I can love this baby!" She went on to say she loved Layton so completely she didn't know how to find room in her heart for that much love, so she was afraid she wouldn't be able to love Holden as completely as she loved our first son. I tried to comfort her and reassure her, but I understood the heart behind what she was saying. Having children is scary, and you always feel completely unqualified and unprepared to do what is in front of you. We get to the hospital, and they begin the process. Now early in this pregnancy, Candice had felt like the Father had wanted her to pray 1 Tim 2:15: *"Nevertheless she will be saved in childbearing if they continue in faith, love, and self-control."* When we were in the hospital room, this prayer was clearly bearing fruit. She was having contractions, but we were watching music videos and resting. The entire labor and delivery were a breeze. The doctor came and checked her around 3 and said it would be a while, and she should sleep if she could. About 15 minutes later, Candice asks me If I would look at the monitor because something seemed different. I couldn't see any changes in the monitor, but I said I would get the nurse. The nurse came in, and while she didn't think there was a need to check, she said she would check just to make sure. The nurse looked and immediately changed gears. They called the doctor who had left to return to his office, and by the time he returned, we were ready to have the baby. Three pushes later we were face to face with this new son who we wanted to love with our whole hearts, and we weren't sure what that would look like until we heard him cry for the first time. Then as Candice would describe it later, we felt our hearts double in size.

Good Pasture

The Good Shepherd lays down his life for the sheep.

If a father's love is finite, then the children are left in competition for that love. My earthly father was a really good dad, but we grew up when he didn't know Jesus. Consequently, while my brother, sister, and I knew he loved us, we were left in a struggle to be the focus of that love. I think each one of us thought dad loved one of our siblings more. This unspoken limit on the love of a father was carried with me into my relationship with my heavenly Father. I wouldn't have had the words to explain it, but I felt an urge to perform for my Father to be worthy of His love. While I knew intellectually His love was unconditional and infinite, my heart felt like I needed to earn my portion as if His love were conditional and finite. This instant doubling of our hearts when Holden was born expressed to me in a way words never could the infinite nature of Agape or God's kind of love. This truth removed the anxiousness I sometimes felt in following my Good Shepherd. Anxious sheep are sheep that are easy for the wolf to scare away. The love of the Father brings peace and security and makes it easier to follow the Good Shepherd.

What I Learned Later

I was like many believers; we may believe God loves us all the same, but we have a nagging suspicion that we are tied for last place when it comes to the Father's love. We will readily answer the question "Does God love you?" with a hearty yes but if then asked in the very next breath if we think God really likes us and we get a little more uncertain. The Father likes his children he doesn't just love them. We were created to walk in the Garden with our creator. He enjoys us! A good earthly father likes his kids, even when those kids sometimes misbehave. How much more does our Heavenly Father enjoy His children even when His children have fallen and made mistakes?

Candice

Candice is incredibly talented at whatever she does. The Father has gifted her in many ways and at times my life was so full of rodeo, schools, building a program at Sky, and with our kids that our lives were left without enough space and time for her to explore all of the gifts talents and abilities the Father placed in her. During a time of prayer, the Father showed me how my life will not be judged only on what I do with the Grace of God placed in me but with how much I have nourished and protected the Grace of God placed in my wife. By intentionally making space for her to spread her wings in whichever way she wants to fly, I make space for the Father to pour out His Grace on and through her. I certainly haven't done this perfectly and it is still an ongoing process, but I am constantly amazed at how beautifully my wife has blossomed even when she is sometimes blossoming in the cracks of my concrete.

My words are too small and too trite to contain the amazing Grace of my heavenly Father which the Father has shown me in her. We are sometimes like a rocky coast along a seashore. A wild place but a place of beauty and power. God gave me the gift of Candice, and my hope is I have not hindered her from becoming all the Father wants her to be. The Good Shepherd is leading her to Good Pasture also and I am excited to see where He takes her and the grace He pours out on her.

GOOD PASTURE

The Father takes us out to Good pasture, but as we mature as sheep some of the greatest moments are watching Him bring other sheep to their Good Pasture. Watching them free to frolic on the mountainsides of the Father's love is rejuvenating and empowering to our own walk. Especially when we see those we knew when we were back in the pen or by the gate. We see those we love expanding and growing in the Love of the Father finding for themselves who they were made to become. Amazing people finding they were built for a life of love, grace, and adventure, a life full of purpose and power. Watching and participating in the Father's plan to lead them to Good pasture is incredibly fulfilling and causes our own walk to be renewed and reinvigorated.

Epilogue

My hope in writing this book was to try, in my limited way, to show the incredible love of the Father for one of His children, and to show the way He wants us to experience it. The Father's love was all that was needed to draw me into a deep relationship with Him. I got to experience His patience as He waited for me to get my belly full of life in the sheep pen. I experienced His kindness as He gave me my desires and waited while I saw they were empty without Him. I experienced how He was never envious even though I had allowed steer wrestling to be more important than Him. I experienced the humble way He waited for me to hang out in the muddy part of the field near the gate as I hesitated to follow the narrow path. I have experienced how He never rudely insisted on His way, but He was always a gentleman leading me along wild and dangerous paths where I would often get scared or hesitant. He was never provoked even though there were times when I would yell or scream at Him to tell me what to do or where to go. I experienced Him taking no joy in my iniquity yet bearing all things for the moment when I would yield. I experienced the way He believed in me even when I had no belief in any part of me, and when I was at my lowest and thought I was only trash He showed me hope in even my lowest pit. He has endured with me through it all, and I have experienced His unfailing, unending, reckless, unfathomable, unbreakable, prodigal love. My hope is this book will help someone else find the Good Shepherd and will encourage them to follow Him to their good pasture, that they too will experience His goodness and love in the here and now.

ABOUT THE AUTHOR

In 2001, Rope Myers became the World Champion Steer Wrestler, smashing the NFR arena average and the record for steer wrestling earnings in one year. He was also the 2002 Gold Medalist at the Olympic Command Performance Rodeo. In 2011, his horsemanship skills offered a new avenue for his competitive spirit—as a contestant on the History Channel's Full Metal Jousting reality show. He's been featured in several national publications, including Sports Illustrated, American Horse, USA Today, Cowboy Sports Entertainment, Western Horseman, Rolling Stone Magazine, and CBS' 48 Hours.

Today Rope lives in east Texas with his wife Candice, where they both serve the ministry of Sky Ranch Christian Camps. The two have four children and, in addition to nearly 25 years of ministry experience, have spent (and continue to spend) a great deal of their time spectating—youth sports, theater productions, junior rodeos ... loving every minute of it.

www.ingramcontent.com/pod-product-compliance
Lightning Source LLC
LaVergne TN
LVHW051244080426
835513LV00016B/1721